3-MINUTE
PRAYERS
FOR BOYS

ISBN 978-1-68322-999-5

Published by Barbour Books, an imprint of Barbour Publishing, Inc., 1810 Barbour Drive, Uhrichsville, Ohio 44683, www.barbourbooks.com

Our mission is to inspire the world with the life-changing message of the Bible.

Member of the
Evangelical Christian
Publishers Association

Printed in the United States of America.
06427 0319 SP

3-MINUTE PRAYERS
FOR BOYS

JOSH MOSEY

BARBOUR BOOKS
An Imprint of Barbour Publishing, Inc.

INTRODUCTION

Never stop praying.
1 THESSALONIANS 5:17

These timely, inspiring prayers are written especially for eight- to twelve-year-old boys, "men under construction" for whom a solid foundation of scripture and prayer will help them weather the storms of life. Guys, just three minutes is all you'll need to charge your spiritual batteries for the busy, happy, scary, or exciting things you'll face each day:

- Minute 1: Read and reflect on God's Word.
- Minute 2: Pray, using the provided prayer to jump-start a conversation with God.
- Minute 3: Reflect on a question or two for further thought.

This book isn't meant to replace your own Bible reading and study. But every one of these scriptures and prayers can help to keep you grounded —focused on the One who hears all your prayers. May this book remind you that the heavenly Father cares about everything you have to say. So go on... talk to Him today. He's ready and waiting to hear from you!

5

CREATIVITY

*God saw all that He had made and it
was very good. There was evening
and there was morning, the sixth day.*
GENESIS 1:31

Creator God, I was made in Your image. Let me be like You today in Your creativity. No one can imagine how incredible You are, but the things You make point us to Your goodness. You have given us life, food, and family. You made people to live in Your garden and have a relationship with You. And even when they messed things up for everyone, You made a way for any of us to come back to You. Thank You for taking care of me, God. You make good things to show us that You care about us. Today, help me make things that are good to show others that I care about You.

Think about it:

What do you think is the most creative
thing God made? What creative thing
can you make or do for someone else?

PEER PRESSURE

Do not act like the sinful people of the world.
Let God change your life. First of all, let Him give
you a new mind. Then you will know what God
wants you to do. And the things you do will be
good and pleasing and perfect.
ROMANS 12:2

Lord, help me to keep my eyes on You. Give me courage to live my life according to Your Word. My friends may judge me for the way I act, but they are not my judge—You are, Lord. Remind me that my mind, my body, and my relationships are Yours to do with what You want. When other people want me to do things that You tell me I shouldn't, help me to be bold. When the things of this world look better than my relationship with You, remind me that I am Yours.

Think about it:

Do your friends help you act more like
God or less like Him? How can you remind
yourself that you belong to God?

TeACHeRS

"The follower is not more important than his teacher.
But everyone who learns well will be like his teacher."
LUKE 6:40

Lord, though it doesn't always feel like it, the fact is that my teachers know more than me. Help me to respect them. Help me to learn what I can from them, to put the same effort into learning that I put into having fun. Someday, it will pay off. I don't know everything yet, but You do—and I know that You put people in leadership over me for reasons that You alone understand. When it feels like my teachers are being harsh, help me see this as another opportunity to learn. Lord, keep me humble and help me grow. May I be more than a student in a classroom. May my attitude and actions teach others what it means to be a Christian.

Think about it:

Do you ever feel like your teachers are unfair? What could you change about yourself to be a better student?

LOYALTY AMONG FRIENDS

A man who has friends must be a friend, but there is a friend who stays nearer than a brother.
PROVERBS 18:24

Lord, real friends don't come easy. A guy can have lots of friends but still not have any close ones. I pray that I can be a loyal friend. You know what it feels like to be betrayed. You know how it feels when someone pretends they don't know You. Lord, help me never betray my friends or act like they don't matter. Remind me that You don't care how many friends I have, but You care about how I treat the friends I have. I pray that my friends come to know You like I do. I pray that You'll help us all know You better. And, Lord, thank You for counting me as Your friend.

Think about it:

When was the last time a friend made you feel like you didn't matter? When was the last time you treated a friend like that?

PRAISING GOD FOR HIS WORKS

I will give thanks to the Lord with all my heart.
I will tell of all the great things You have done.
I will be glad and full of joy because of You.
I will sing praise to Your name, O Most High.
PSALM 9:1–2

Amazing God, You are definitely worthy of praise. You created everything from nothing. You know my needs before I do and You provide for each one. You give freely, even though I cannot repay You. You bless me with family and friends who love me. You forgive me when I mess up. You speak to me through Your Word. You give my life purpose and value. You invite me to come near to You. No matter how many times I run away, You welcome me back with open arms. Lord, I don't deserve the kindness You show me. Thank You.

Think about it:

What are some specific things God has done for you? What does it mean to be "full of joy" in God?

HYPOCRISY

"Why do you look at the small piece of wood in your brother's eye and do not see the big piece of wood in your own eye? How can you say to your brother, 'Let me take that small piece of wood out of your eye,' when you do not see the big piece of wood in your own eye?... First, take the big piece of wood out of your own eye. Then you can see better to take the small piece of wood out of your brother's eye."

LUKE 6:41–42

Lord, forgive me for the times when I act like I have my act together. I know I am not perfect. Only You are. Only You have the clear vision and awesome power to help me see more clearly. Help me approach You and other people with a humble heart.

Think about it:

Is it possible you have a blind spot in your spiritual life? Would you ask God to point it out to you?

THE PEACE OF GOD

*"Peace I leave with you. My peace I give to you.
I do not give peace to you as the world gives.
Do not let your hearts be troubled or afraid."*
JOHN 14:27

Lord, I need to feel Your peace today. I hear people talk about scary things happening in the world. Sometimes, my life can be kind of scary too. But no matter how frightening this world can be, I know You are in control. Lord, help me put my worries and fears into Your hands. Help me trust You more, in every area of my life. May the things that worry me fade away when I listen for the whisper of Your presence. Lord, I pray for the calm that only You can give.

Think about it:

What kinds of things worry you? Do you
believe that God has things under control?
Is there someone, like a parent, you can
talk to about scary news in the world?

TREATING GIRLS WITH RESPECT

My true helper, I ask you to help these women who have worked with me so much in preaching the Good News to others. Clement helped also. There are others who worked with me. Their names are in the book of life.
PHILIPPIANS 4:3

Creator God, You made both men and women in Your image. Lord, whenever I am tempted to treat girls disrespectfully, remind me that they are my fellow workers whose names are in the book of life. Remind me that You value them as highly as You value me. Remind me that when I disrespect them, I am disrespecting a person who was made in Your image. Help me see all people as You see them: as someone You came to save. May I see an opportunity today to treat girls with the respect and kindness You show to me.

Think about it:

How do you treat girls? Are you respectful?
Does what they look like affect
how you treat them?

BeING HATeD

"If the world hates you, you know it hated Me before it hated you."
JOHN 15:18

Lord, I know that not everyone has to like me. But if someone doesn't like me, please let that be for the right reasons. If someone dislikes me because I act and talk like You, I pray that person will come to know You. If someone dislikes me because I am *not* acting and talking like You, I pray that I might be forgiven and that I can change how I act and talk. Help me to not respond to hate with hate. You know what it is to be hated, and You loved us in spite of it. Lord, make me more like You, even if that means some people won't like me. Your love for me outweighs the hate of the world. Thank You for loving me.

Think about it:

When someone dislikes you, is it because you are acting like Christ? Do you answer hate with love? What would that look like?

OVERCOMING TEMPTATION

*You have never been tempted to sin in any different
way than other people. God is faithful. He will not
allow you to be tempted more than you can take.
But when you are tempted, He will make a way
for you to keep from falling into sin.*
1 CORINTHIANS 10:13

Faithful God, sometimes I feel like doing things I
know I shouldn't do. I know everyone gets tempted,
but I also know that what I want isn't always what
is best for me. I pray that You'll change my wants
so they'll be what You want for me. You tell me I
won't be tempted beyond what I can handle, but I
can't handle anything without You. Lord, help me
not try to resist temptations on my own. Thank You
for making a way for me to resist the things I know
are wrong. Help me see You instead of what I think
I want.

Think about it:

What kinds of things tempt you?
Have you given those things to God?

Getting Along with Others

Work for the things that make peace and help each other become stronger Christians.
Romans 14:19

Lord, help me get along with people around me. If I'm doing something that bothers others, please help me see it and stop it. I'd rather get along with people and show them love than get my own way. Lord, help me find ways to build people up rather than tear them down. Help me see the needs of others more clearly than what I want. I pray for opportunities today to show kindness, whether it is to my family or my friends or someone I don't even like that much. Help me be an example of the love You had for me before I came to love You. Help me bring a bit of peace to this crazy world.

Think about it:

What does it look like to build someone up instead of tearing them down? What is something you do that you know bothers someone else? What could you do instead?

AMAZING GRACE

What I say is true and all the world should receive it. Christ Jesus came into the world to save sinners from their sin and I am the worst sinner.
1 TIMOTHY 1:15

Gracious God, I'm so glad You sent Jesus to save sinners. If I had to save myself, I'd be in real trouble. You didn't come to save just people who have sinned a little. You came to save the very worst of us. Thank You for saving me from every selfish thought, every bad word, every mean thing I've done. Thank You for saving me from sins I haven't even committed yet. Your grace really is amazing. Help me always accept the forgiveness You freely give. Help me to forgive other people just like You've forgiven me.

Think about it:

Do you ever feel like you've done too many bad things to be saved? What does the verse above tell you about that? Do you show others the same grace God has shown you?

BAD HAIR DAYS

Do not let your beauty come from the outside.
It should not be the way you comb your hair or the
wearing of gold or the wearing of fine clothes. Your
beauty should come from the inside. It should come
from the heart. This is the kind that lasts. Your
beauty should be a gentle and quiet spirit.
1 PETER 3:3–4

Father God, sometimes when I wake up and look in the mirror, I can't help but feel like it's going to be a bad day. My hair is a mess and my clothes don't look right. I know You look at what's going on inside my heart, but everyone else looks at what is outside. Lord, help me get my priorities straight. If people make fun of me for my looks today, help me love them anyway. And thanks for loving me, even on bad hair days.

Think about it:

Do you ever judge people based on their appearance? What could you do for someone whose appearance isn't what others think it should be?

HARD WORK VS. LAZINESS

The soul of the lazy person has strong desires
but gets nothing, but the soul of the one who
does his best gets more than he needs.
PROVERBS 13:4

Lord, I could probably fill an entire page with the things I want. But I know that wanting and getting are two different things. Lord, first help me want the right things. Help me value You and Your desires more than new video games or clothes or sports gear. Then, once my priorities are straight, help me be willing to work hard and keep working hard. Help me not to put things off when I can and should do them now. Help me build a reputation as a hard worker, not only for myself but as a reflection of my love for You.

Think about it:

Who do you know who works hard all the time?
When was the last time you did what was asked
of you right away and kept at it until it was done?

I'M TOO YOUNG!

Now the Word of the Lord came to me saying... "Before you were born, I set you apart as holy. I chose you to speak to the nations for Me." Then I said, "O, Lord God! I do not know how to speak. I am only a boy." But the Lord said to me, "Do not say, 'I am only a boy.' You must go everywhere I send you. And you must say whatever I tell you. Do not be afraid of them. For I am with you to take you out of trouble."
JEREMIAH 1:4–8

Lord, I am young, but I'm not too young to do what You tell me to do. I may not know the words to say, but I trust that You'll help me. Give me the courage I need to follow Your commands. Thank You for choosing me to do Your work.

Think about it:

What is God asking you to do for Him today? Are you willing to do it?

WANTING TO BE COOL

*So put away all pride from yourselves. You are
standing under the powerful hand of God.
At the right time He will lift you up.*
1 PETER 5:6

Father God, I admit that I want to be cool. I want
other people to like me. I want to have lots of
friends and to always be picked first for teams. And
although I don't think it's wrong to be well liked,
I know I shouldn't focus on whether or not people
think I'm cool. After all, You are the God of the entire universe, and You chose me to be Yours. That's
a lot cooler than I deserve! Lord, help me be patient
and focus less on myself. May I wait for You to lift
me up at the right time.

Think about it:

Do you ever feel tempted to do things you
shouldn't just so people will like you more?
How does it make you feel that the all-powerful
God of the universe has chosen you to be His?

BEING A MAN OF YOUR WORD

*"Let your yes be YES. Let your no be NO.
Anything more than this comes from the devil."*
MATTHEW 5:37

Trustworthy God, I pray that I will do the things I've said I will do, that I will avoid the things I have said I will not do, and that people will trust me because I have proven myself trustworthy. I know You are in control of every situation and that I can't change anything You have decided. I pray that my intentions and my efforts are part of Your plan. I will do my best to keep my word, but when I say I'll do something You don't have planned for me, remind me that Your plan is best. Lord, as much as it is in my power, help me grow to be a man of my word.

Think about it:

How do you feel when someone says they'll
do something for you and then they don't?
Do you ever say you'll do something,
then change your mind?

STARTING GOSSIP

*He who covers a sin looks for love. He who
tells of trouble separates good friends.*
PROVERBS 17:9

Lord, it is no fun when someone hurts me, even
when it's not on purpose. When I'm hurt, it's hard to
forgive someone who has hurt me. It is a whole lot
easier to tell my friends about it, so they'll also be
mad at the person who hurt me. But You tell me that
spreading my hurts around is wrong. I can't pretend
that person didn't hurt me, but I can forgive him.
Lord, help me forgive like You do. You never throw
it back in my face when I do something that hurts
You. You just forgive me and we move on. Help me
show Your love and keep my friendships strong.

Think about it:

Have you ever told another person that someone
has hurt you without trying to work things out
with that person first? How does that kind of
gossip affect your relationship with your friends?

GOD'S GOOD PURPOSE

*We know that God makes all things work
together for the good of those who love Him
and are chosen to be a part of His plan.*
ROMANS 8:28

Lord, I usually hear people quote the verse above when things don't go according to their own plans. When bad things happen, people like to say that all things work together for good, as though that makes the bad things less bad. Lord, I know Your plan is perfect, so when bad things happen to me, remind me that it doesn't mean things aren't going according to Your plan. I may not understand why things happen, but I know You have good reasons for the bad things and the good things. Help me see things like You do.

Think about it:

When bad things happen to you, do you feel like God is losing control? Is it easier for you to trust God when good things happen? How can you still show love to God when bad things happen?

TIME MANAGEMENT

Teach us to understand how many days we have.
Then we will have a heart of wisdom to give You.
PSALM 90:12

Eternal God, with my whole life before me, it is easy to think there will be time later for the things I should be doing now. You've given everyone a limited amount of time on this earth to get things done. I pray that You'll help me use my time wisely, whether I live to be a hundred, or whether I die tomorrow. Help me understand which things are important to You so I can do those first. Help me resist the things I want to do just because I want to do them. Give me the joy that comes with knowing that I've done the right thing at the right time.

Think about it:

Do you use your time on the things that
are important to you or on the things that
are important to God? How do you think
you'll be able to tell the difference?

FAKE NEWS

Do not laugh at those who speak for God.
Test everything and do not let good
things get away from you.
1 THESSALONIANS 5:20–21

God of all truth, I hear a lot of things throughout the day, and sometimes the things I hear don't make sense. One side says one thing, and another side says the opposite. I need Your wisdom to help me know what is true and right. Help me not to believe everything I hear without seeking out the truth from the Bible. Help me to test the things people say against what You have shown me to be true. And when I know that something is untrue, teach me to be kind to the person who disagrees. I pray that Your love will flow through me and help others see Your truth.

Think about it:

Do you test the things you hear from others,
or do you believe people just because they
tell you they are right? How can you tell
what is true and what is false?

PERSONAL RESPONSIBILITY

*Do not be fooled. You cannot fool God. A man will
get back whatever he plants! If a man does things
to please his sinful old self, his soul will be lost.
If a man does things to please the Holy Spirit,
he will have life that lasts forever.*
GALATIANS 6:7–8

Lord, I've grown up with people taking care of me
and being responsible for me. But I realize that as I
grow, I'll be more and more responsible for myself.
If I do things I shouldn't do, I will face the consequences. And if I do the things I should be doing,
I will be rewarded. Lord, I can't do the right things
without You living inside of me and acting through
me. I pray that I won't get tired of letting You work
in me and through me.

Think about it:

Do you sometimes let yourself believe there
won't be consequences for doing bad things?
What are the rewards for doing the right thing?

OUR POWERFUL GOD

*"O Lord God! See, You have made the heavens
and the earth by Your great power and by
Your long arm! Nothing is too hard for You!"*
JEREMIAH 32:17

Powerful God, there is nothing You cannot do! You are the Creator, but You didn't stop at creation. You take care of me, from before I was born until after I die, and then forever after that. Nothing can stand in Your way and nothing can slow You down. No problem is so big that You can't solve it, and no problem is so small that You don't care about it. Thank You for being not only powerful, but powerfully good. What a scary thing it would be to live in a world with an all-powerful God who didn't love His creation! Thank You for caring about all my problems, both big and small.

Think about it:

What things about God amaze you?
What is the biggest problem in your life right now? Do you believe God can solve it?

eASY PReY?

Keep awake! Watch at all times. The devil is working against you. He is walking around like a hungry lion with his mouth open. He is looking for someone to eat.
1 PETER 5:8

Lord, help me see and avoid the traps the devil has set for me. Keep me from being easy prey for the sin that hunts for me. Lord, as my selfish desires roar for attention, I pray that You will lock their jaws tight. Any time I try to take on the devil by myself, I fail. I need Your help to hunt down the things that hunt me. Lord, I put myself in Your hands so I don't end up in the devil's jaws. Thank You for rescuing me from every trap, every roar, every lion. Every time.

Think about it:

Do you ever feel like sin is hunting you? When you hear the roar of something you know you shouldn't do, how do you fight it?

MEMBERS OF GOD'S FAMILY

From now on you are not strangers and people who are not citizens. You are citizens together with those who belong to God. You belong in God's family. This family is built on the teachings of the missionaries and the early preachers. Jesus Christ Himself is the cornerstone, which is the most important part of the building.

EPHESIANS 2:19–20

Father God, thank You for welcoming me into Your family. When other people look at me, may they see a brother. When I meet other people, help me to treat them like family. Help me see beyond skin color and hear beyond accents and language barriers. Remind me to never make Your people feel like outsiders or strangers. Give me the humility to see that You are the reason that I'm in this family at all.

Think about it:

When you see someone who looks different from you, do you see them as family? How would you treat people differently if you could see them as God sees them?

KEEP ON KNOCKING

"Ask, and what you are asking for will be given to you. Look, and what you are looking for you will find. Knock, and the door you are knocking on will be opened to you."
MATTHEW 7:7

Lord, when I pray for something, it is easy to get discouraged when I don't get it right away. It might be that You are telling me I'm not going to get what I ask for, but it might also be that You are waiting for me to ask again. Give me the wisdom to tell the difference. When I feel like giving up too early, encourage me to stick with it. You want to open the door for me when I ask for the right things, so keep me from being distracted while I knock. Keep me from trying to open the door by force.

Think about it:

Have you ever asked God for something once, then given up? What keeps you from continuing to knock until God answers you?

WORDS THAT CUT

There is one whose foolish words cut like a sword,
but the tongue of the wise brings healing.
PROVERBS 12:18

Lord, sometimes words hurt. When people say unkind things to me, they have hurt me on purpose. But sometimes words can hurt even when a person doesn't mean them to. You say that foolish words cut like a sword, and that makes sense to me. Lord, help me be wise with my words. May they bring healing instead of pain. And when someone uses cutting words against me, I pray that I won't try to hurt that person back. Just as I need to be careful whenever I use something sharp, I need to be careful with what I say. Help me to forgive, because I know that if I'm not careful with my words, I could end up just hurting myself.

Think about it:

Are you careful with what you say to or
about other people? How could your
own words come back to hurt you?

STRENGTH IN WEAKNESS

He answered me, "I am all you need. I give you My loving-favor. My power works best in weak people." I am happy to be weak and have troubles so I can have Christ's power in me.
2 CORINTHIANS 12:9

Lord, You see right through me when I pretend I am fine. You know when I feel broken and weak, but my weakness is an opportunity for You to show Your strength. Lord, I need Your strength because I'm not fine all the time. Rather than putting on a brave face and powering through my day, I need to let Your power live in me. Help me be honest with others about how I'm feeling and about the things I'm going through. Help me to not pressure myself into being something I'm not. You've promised to love me, even when I'm weak. Thank You for Your love and power.

Think about it:

Do you ever try to hide your weaknesses? Who is someone you can talk with when you feel weak?

HIDDEN TALENTS

God has given each of you a gift. Use it to help each other. This will show God's loving-favor. If a man preaches, let him do it with God speaking through him. If a man helps others, let him do it with the strength God gives. So in all things God may be honored through Jesus Christ. Shining-greatness and power belong to Him forever. Let it be so.

1 PETER 4:10–11

Generous God, You have given me lots of gifts and talents. I pray that You would help me use them for You. It is tempting to do things I'm good at so people will tell me how great I am. But I know that's not why You gave me my abilities. Remind me often that You deserve the praise, not me. Let others see You more than me.

Think about it:

How do you feel when someone tells you that you are good at something? What are some ways you can use your talents for God?

HONOR YOUR PARENTS

*"Honor your father and your mother, so your life may
be long in the land the Lord your God gives you."*
EXODUS 20:12

Heavenly Father, when You gave Your followers the rules they needed to follow, You didn't tell them why they shouldn't murder people or lie. But when it came to the commandment to honor their parents, You gave them a reason and a promise. You promised a whole nation of people long lives and a special place just for obeying this one law, so I figure there must be something life-giving about obeying my parents and treating them with respect. It isn't always easy to honor my parents. They make lots of mistakes, just like I do. So help me treat my parents with the respect they deserve, not because they are perfect, but because You are and You tell me I should.

Think about it:

Why do you think it is important to
God that kids honor their parents?
How can you honor your parents today?

WHAT CAN ANYONE DO TO ME?

In God I have put my trust. I will not
be afraid. What can man do to me?
PSALM 56:11

All-powerful God, I pray that I will always trust You and love You. When bad things happen to me, help me turn to You for comfort. That may not always be easy, but help me be bold in my commitment to You. When others make fun of me or threaten me for following You, help me see things like You see them. Help me choose to love, even as I'm being hurt. You did, and You call me to be like You. People can do all kinds of bad things to me because I follow You. But no one could ever separate me from Your love. So give me the courage to always stand with You and for You, no matter what.

Think about it:

Do people ever threaten or ridicule you
for your faith in God? How did Jesus
handle it when He was threatened?

WAITING

"Do not let your heart be troubled. You have put your trust in God, put your trust in Me also. There are many rooms in My Father's house. If it were not so, I would have told you. I am going away to make a place for you. After I go and make a place for you, I will come back and take you with Me. Then you may be where I am."
JOHN 14:1–3

Lord, it's hard waiting for the things I want. Waiting is never fun, but it seems hardest when I don't know how long I'll be waiting. Lord, I pray for patience while I wait. Give me a good attitude and help me to be useful. You know what it is like to wait, since You are waiting to come back for us. I trust You and Your timing, both for the small things and the big things I've asked for.

Think about it:

What are you waiting for right now?
How can you make the wait worthwhile?

THE INTERNET

Christian brothers, keep your minds thinking about whatever is true, whatever is respected, whatever is right, whatever is pure, whatever can be loved, and whatever is well thought of. If there is anything good and worth giving thanks for, think about these things.
PHILIPPIANS 4:8

Lord, the internet is a wild and crazy place. It's a useful tool I can use to chat with friends and do homework, but there are a lot of nasty things on there too. Whether it's sites I know I shouldn't go to, or people on social media I know would drag me down, help me be wise with my eyes. I need Your help to focus on the things that are true, honorable, right, pure, lovely, and admirable. Help my actions online be a good example to my friends and family.

Think about it:

When you go online, do you focus on things that are honorable and pure? Do your social media posts show your friends and family that you love God?

RESPECTING AUTHORITY

Every person must obey the leaders of the land. There is no power given but from God, and all leaders are allowed by God.
ROMANS 13:1

Lord, I hear news about the government all the time. Whenever my friends and family members talk about the people in charge, someone gets upset. I know You are in control of everything and that You have put certain people in charge. But sometimes it's hard for me to understand why You allow some people to lead. Lord, help me obey the rules the leaders set up. If I disobey the rules that have been set up to protect me, I put myself at risk of getting into trouble. Help me obey because I want to follow You, no matter how I feel about the person in authority. Thank You for being in charge.

Think about it:

Is it ever hard for you to obey the rules? If you broke the rules, how would your disobedience reflect on you, your family, and God?

THE SWORD OF GOD'S WORD

God's Word is living and powerful. It is sharper than
a sword that cuts both ways. It cuts straight into
where the soul and spirit meet and it divides them.
It cuts into the joints and bones. It tells what the
heart is thinking about and what it wants to do.
HEBREWS 4:12

Father God, You are the Author of the living book, the Bible. Your Word has the power to hurt and to save. Lord, I pray that Your Word will correct me when I need it, no matter how much it hurts. I thank You that Your Word also heals me as it brings me closer to You. Help me not use Your Word as a weapon against others, but as a tool to bring healing. May I live true to the message of Your goodness.

Think about it:

Why is it important to take God's Word
seriously? How do you respond when
something you read in the Bible hurts?

GIVE THANKS FOR
GOD'S GOODNESS

O give thanks to the Lord, for He is good.
His loving-kindness lasts forever.
1 CHRONICLES 16:34

Loving God, thank You for Your goodness and love. You could have made anything, and You chose to make me. Thank You for making me. You could have filled this world with monsters and unbreathable air, but You made this world beautiful instead. Thank You for Your creation. You could have made it so people just popped into being one at a time, but You gave us a family to love us and teach us about You. Thank You for my family. And when I mess up and do things I know You don't like, You could punish me, but You forgive me instead. Thank You for forgiving me. Everywhere I look, I see hundreds of different examples that show that You love me. Thank You for Your love!

Think about it:

What are some examples of God's goodness in your life? How can you tell that He loves you?

EVERY LITTLE THING

*So if you eat or drink or whatever
you do, do everything to honor God.*
1 CORINTHIANS 10:31

Glorious God, I am all Yours. I pray that everything I do, I do because I want to honor You. I want every little thing I do to be about You and for You. Help me keep You in the front of my mind as I do even the most simple things every day. When I get out of bed, let me thank You for the sunrise. When I eat my breakfast, let me thank You for the food You've provided. When I do my chores or my homework, let me thank You for the muscles and brains You gave me. And help me use those muscles and brains to do the things that You like best. Show me how I can honor You every day.

Think about it:

What does it mean to you to honor God?
How can you remind yourself every day
to honor Him in everything you do?

JUDGING APPEARANCES

*But the Lord said to Samuel, "Do not look at the way
he looks on the outside or how tall he is, because I
have not chosen him. For the Lord does not look at
the things man looks at. A man looks at the outside
of a person, but the Lord looks at the heart."*
1 SAMUEL 16:7

Lord, help me to always see past how a person looks
on the outside. It is really easy to look at people and
think I know what they are like. But only You know
what a person is really like. Lord, give me Your eyes
and help me see people for who they really are. And
may I not show love based on how someone looks,
but on how much that person needs it.

Think about it:

What assumptions do you make about how
people should look? How do you treat or
think of people who don't look the way you
think they should? How do you think
God chooses people to do His will?

MONEY, MONEY, MONEY

The love of money is the beginning of all kinds
of sin. Some people have turned from the faith
because of their love for money. They have made
much pain for themselves because of this.
1 TIMOTHY 6:10

Lord, I know that money itself isn't evil. But I also know that people sometimes go a little crazy because they want more money. People steal it. They do bad things to earn it. Some even kill other people over it. Lord, I pray that I would always love You more than money. I pray that I would see money as a tool to take care of my basic needs and to show others kindness. Whether I have a lot of money or a little, remind me to always be generous with what I have. Keep me from causing my own problems because of money.

Think about it:

Do you see money as a tool to get the things you want or as a means to bless people around you?

STICK WITH IT

*Watch yourselves! You do not want to lose
what we have worked for. You want to
get what has been promised to you.*
2 JOHN 8

Lord, You never quit when You are halfway finished with something. You didn't half create the world. You didn't rest until You were done. Lord, help me be like You so I don't stop early. Help me stick with it until I've finished the job. When I don't feel like finishing my work because I would rather play, help me refocus so I can get the job done. If I stop before I finish, I might as well have not started at all. Help me do a good job so that when it is done, I can rest and relax without worrying about what I still need to finish. Thank You for being a finisher, God.

Think about it:

Do you sometimes find it hard to finish
something you've started? What is
the reward for not giving up?

WHAT IS LOVE?

Love does not give up. Love is kind. Love is not jealous.
Love does not put itself up as being important. Love
has no pride. Love does not do the wrong thing.
Love never thinks of itself. Love does not get angry.
Love does not remember the suffering that comes
from being hurt by someone. Love is not happy
with sin. Love is happy with the truth.
1 CORINTHIANS 13:4–6

Loving God, I have trouble loving like I'm supposed to. I'm not always patient or kind. I find it hard not to want what other people have. I like it when people pay attention to me. Honestly, I'm kind of rude sometimes, and I get angry when I don't get my own way. Lord, change my heart so I can love like I'm supposed to. Help me be patient and kind. Help me focus less on myself and my wants and more on other people.

Think about it:

How can you show love today? How do you
react when you don't get what you want?

GeT TOGeTHeR

Let us help each other to love others and to do good.
Let us not stay away from church meetings. Some
people are doing this all the time. Comfort each
other as you see the day of His return coming near.
HEBREWS 10:24–25

Lord, sometimes I don't feel like going to church.
You tell me it is important, but sometimes I just
can't get into the music or the teaching. Help me
see church as a place where I can be encouraged
and where I can encourage other people. Lord, let
me see the needs of the people at church and do
what I can to take care of them. Let me see church
as a chance to give back. Help me learn more about
You while I'm there, and help me use that knowledge to serve You better.

Think about it:

How do you see church? Is it boring or exciting?
Is church there to take care of you, or is it a
place where you can take care of others?

QUICK TO LISTEN, SLOW TO SPEAK

My Christian brothers, you know everyone
should listen much and speak little.
He should be slow to become angry.
JAMES 1:19

Patient God, You made me with two ears and one mouth, but sometimes I talk twice as much as I listen. I pray that I would listen before I speak when I have disagreements and misunderstandings with my friends and family members. When someone says something hurtful, I pray that You would help me not get angry. I pray for a peaceful spirit like Yours so that I don't make things worse by answering anger with anger. Thank You for being patient with me. Thank You for always listening when I need to talk. Help me show other people the same kindness and patience You show to me.

Think about it:

When you have a misunderstanding with someone, do you stop and listen or do you get louder? How can you stop yourself before you say something you might regret?

FORGETFUL FORGIVENESS

"I will show loving-kindness to them and forgive their sins. I will remember their sins no more."
HEBREWS 8:12

Forgiving God, a day doesn't go by without me messing up in some way. But no matter how sinful and selfish I am, You never throw it back in my face after I ask for forgiveness. You forgive me every time. But when someone else does something mean to me, I have a hard time letting it go, even after that person asks for forgiveness. Lord, help me forgive like You do. Help me to forget the mean things others have done to me. Help me forget even my own failings, so I can live free in the joy of Your forgiveness. Thank You for forgiving and forgetting.

Think about it:

What would it look like to truly forgive and forget when someone is mean to you? Do you ever have trouble forgiving and forgetting your own sins after you've asked God to forgive you?

WHEN FRIENDS ARGUE

Sharp words spoken in the open are better than love that is hidden. The pains given by a friend are faithful, but the kisses of one who hates you are false.
PROVERBS 27:5–6

Lord, thank You for my friends. Even though we can sometimes be mean to each other, I know they are still my friends. Lord, help me be a good and faithful friend. Help me to never act as though I like someone and then say mean things about him behind his back. I pray that when my friends and I argue, things cool down quickly so that our friendship can get back to normal. Help us work past whatever made us argue in the first place. Lord, thank You for being my Friend and for being genuine and faithful to me.

Think about it:

How do you feel when someone is mean to you behind your back but nice to your face? What can you do to make up with your friends after an argument?

THE LORD'S PRAYER

"Pray like this: 'Our Father in heaven, Your name is holy. May Your holy nation come. What You want done, may it be done on earth as it is in heaven. Give us the bread we need today. Forgive us our sins as we forgive those who sin against us. Do not let us be tempted, but keep us from sin. Your nation is holy. You have power and shining-greatness forever. Let it be so.'"

MATTHEW 6:9–13

Thank You, Lord, for teaching me how to pray. Thank You for telling me what's important to You. Thank You for loving me, for taking care of me, for forgiving me, and for protecting me. May I work hard to bring Your kingdom to this world by showing others the kindness, love, and forgiveness You have shown to me.

Think about it:

What do you think it means to have God's holy nation come? Why do you think Jesus taught His disciples to pray like this?

HOMEWORK

*Listen to words about what you should do,
and take your punishment if you need it,
so that you may be wise the rest of your days.*
PROVERBS 19:20

Lord, give me a thirst for knowledge. Help me see homework assignments as an opportunity to learn and not just a task that needs done. I pray that I'd be able to understand what my teachers are trying to teach me. I pray that I'd be able to apply the knowledge I'm getting. Lord, help me become wise. May I be bold enough to raise my hand in class and ask questions when I don't understand something. I pray that others wouldn't look down on me for not knowing something, but that they would understand that I'm just trying to learn. Lord, help me learn quickly. May I never judge someone else for the things they don't know.

Think about it:

What do you think of having to do homework?
Are you ever afraid someone might judge
you if you ask questions in class?

See A Need, Fill A Need

*We are His work. He has made us to belong
to Christ Jesus so we can work for Him.
He planned that we should do this.*
EPHESIANS 2:10

Father God, You are the Master Planner. You didn't make things by accident. You have a reason for everything You do. Thank You for saving me and including me in Your plan. As I go through my day, help me see the good things You've planned for me to do. Give me Your eyes to see the needs around me. Give me Your strength to fill them. It's incredible to me that You made me so I can do good things. You could have made someone else for the job, but You made me. Thank You. Lord, I pray that You will get the glory for the needs I fill today.

Think about it:

How does it make you feel to know you are part of God's plan? What is a need that you can fill today?

WHO ARE YOU TRYING TO IMPRESS?

*Do you think I am trying to get the favor of men,
or of God? If I were still trying to please men,
I would not be a servant owned by Christ.*

GALATIANS 1:10

Father God, I know it shouldn't matter what other people think about me. You made me and I am Yours. But I still find myself trying to impress my friends. Sometimes, I do things I know I shouldn't do in order to make them laugh or think I'm cool. But I know that isn't how I should try to impress people. Maybe the type of people who are impressed by silly things aren't the type of people I should be hanging out with. Lord, give me the wisdom to know how to act and who to impress. Let me only care what You think about me.

Think about it:

Do you ever do silly things to impress
your friends? What kinds of silly things
do you think God approves of?

HONORING THE ELDERLY

*"Show respect to the person with white hair.
Honor an older person and you will
honor your God. I am the Lord."*
LEVITICUS 19:32

Lord, everyone has worth to You. You made us in Your image. I know I should show love to everyone, but sometimes that isn't easy with old people. They smell weird. They say strange things. Sometimes they look funny. I don't always feel comfortable around them. Lord, I pray that You'd change my heart about the people I'm uncomfortable loving. Help me look past the way they look and smell to see the person You've created. Lord, some old people have great stories and are really funny, but I won't find that out until I talk to them. Give me the courage and kindness I need to show them the respect You've asked me to show.

Think about it:

When is the last time you talked to an elderly person who isn't your grandparent? What could you do today to show an elderly person respect?

BeING ANGRY

If you are angry, do not let it become sin.
Get over your anger before the day is finished.
Do not let the devil start working in your life.
EPHESIANS 4:26–27

Lord, sometimes when people are mean to me or when I get hurt, I get so angry that I just want to punch something. Sometimes, I'm angry for just a second. Other times, I stay angry for a long time. And sometimes, old things pop into my head and I get angry all over again. I don't think anger is a sin, but I know holding on to my anger isn't okay with You. Lord, when I get angry with someone, help it not be for a long time. Help me to work things out with that person quickly so I'm not tempted to do things I shouldn't. Lord, help me forgive and move on, just like You do.

Think about it:

Are you angry about anything right now? What would it take for you to let go of that anger?

MY GROUP OF FRIENDS

My Christian brothers, our Lord Jesus Christ is the Lord of shining-greatness. Since your trust is in Him, do not look on one person as more important than another.
JAMES 2:1

Lord, my group of friends is special to me. It is tempting to treat other kids differently, like they are outsiders to my group, but You tell me not to do that. You love them just as much as You love me. If they believe in You, they are actually my brothers and sisters. It isn't wrong for me to have close friends, but it's not okay when my group excludes other kids because they aren't as cool or don't look like us. Lord, help me be nice to everyone. Help me be a good influence on my friends. And if my friends treat others poorly, let me be brave enough to stand up to them.

Think about it:

Have you ever felt left out by other kids?
How can you treat everyone equally?

PRAY EXPECTANTLY

"For sure, I tell you, a person may say to this mountain, 'Move from here into the sea.' And if he does not doubt, but believes that what he says will be done, it will happen. Because of this, I say to you, whatever you ask for when you pray, have faith that you will receive it. Then you will get it."

MARK 11:23–24

Lord, I pray that my faith in You would be strong enough to move mountains. I believe that You are able to do the most difficult things with ease, but I don't always believe that You will do them for me. Lord, help me have more faith in the plan that You have for me. If it is Your plan to move mountains, give me the boldness I need to ask You to move them.

Think about it:

Do you expect God to answer your prayers? How would you pray differently if you knew that God would do what you are asking?

IT'S OKAY TO CRY SOMETIMES

Then Jesus cried.
JOHN 11:35

Comforting Father, it seems like it's a rule that boys aren't supposed to cry. It doesn't matter if we are feeling hurt or if we lose someone that we're close to, when boys cry, they get called names. But You cried and no one teased You for it. You cried when Your friend died, even though You knew You could bring him back to life. If it is okay for You to cry when You are sad, it must be okay for me too. Lord, let me cry when I need to without worrying what others think. When people who are special to me die, I know I'll see them again if they believed in You. But I still feel sad about it. Thank You for comforting me and for showing me it's okay to cry when I need to.

Think about it:

Have you ever felt like you needed to hide your emotions from others? Do you think you need to hide them from God?

GIFTS + LOVE

I may be able to speak the languages of men and even of angels, but if I do not have love, it will sound like noisy brass. If I have the gift of speaking God's Word and if I understand all secrets, but do not have love, I am nothing. If I know all things and if I have the gift of faith so I can move mountains, but do not have love, I am nothing. If I give everything I have to feed poor people and if I give my body to be burned, but do not have love, it will not help me.
1 CORINTHIANS 13:1–3

Loving God, You gave me some pretty cool gifts and abilities. But no matter how gifted I am, if I am not using my gifts to show love to others, I might as well not have them. Lord, thank You for Your love. Help me love like You do.

Think about it:

How can you use your gifts
to show someone else love?

VOLUNTEERING

Then I heard the voice of the Lord, saying,
"Whom should I send? Who will go for Us?"
Then I said, "Here am I. Send me!"
ISAIAH 6:8

Lord, let me listen well enough to hear the call to volunteer, whether it comes from a teacher, a youth group leader, or straight from You. Then, Lord, I pray that I will be bold enough to say what Isaiah said: "Send me!" I pray that my willingness to do the task comes from a desire to serve, not so that others will think I'm something special. The best thing about me is that You love me and volunteered to take the punishment that I deserve. The least I can do is to serve You with a pure heart. Lord, show me where You want me to volunteer.

Think about it:

What do you usually do when someone asks for a volunteer? When you do volunteer, is it because you want to serve or because you want others to think you're something special?

DEFY THE LABELS

Let no one show little respect for you because you are young. Show other Christians how to live by your life. They should be able to follow you in the way you talk and in what you do. Show them how to live in faith and in love and in holy living.
1 TIMOTHY 4:12

Lord, sometimes, adults put younger people into certain categories without getting to know them. Lord, I pray that I won't be easy to fit into any of these categories. When adults think that all kids are loud and impatient, let me listen and wait. When adults think that all kids are self-centered and greedy, let me be generous with my time, talents, and things. Lord, may my actions and love give adults a reason to look again before they stick a label on me.

Think about it:

What do people think of when they hear your name? Do you give adults a reason to believe that all young people are self-centered, or do they see God's love in you?

PROCRASTINATION

*"You must be ready also. The Son of Man is coming
at a time when you do not think He will come."*
LUKE 12:40

Lord, sometimes I don't feel like doing what needs to be done, so I put it off. It might be because I think the job will be hard, or because I just don't feel like doing it. But I know it isn't good to procrastinate. If I put off cleaning my room, my parents might clean it for me and I might lose the things that made it dirty. If I'm angry with someone and I put off making things right, our relationship might never get better. And if I have sin I haven't confessed, then my relationship with You can't be right either. Lord, help me not put off the important things.

Think about it:

Is there something you need to do but
have been putting off? Is there someone
you've been avoiding, but you know
the relationship needs to be fixed?

BEING KNOWN BY GOD

*But now that you know God, or should I say that you are
known by God, why do you turn back again to the weak
old Law? Why do you want to do those religious acts of
worship that will keep you from being free? Why do you
want to be held under the power of the Law again?*
GALATIANS 4:9

Almighty God, it would be pretty cool to meet a
rock star or a movie star or my favorite author, but
those people are nothing compared with You. To
think that You know me personally and love me
deeply blows my mind. There are so many people
in the world, but still You make time for me. Lord,
I pray that I will value our relationship as highly
as You do. May I never take Your love for granted.
Thank You for choosing to love me.

Think about it:

Think of someone you love very deeply
and personally. How does it feel knowing
God knows and loves *you* personally?

YOUR TRUE HOME

*"My followers do not belong to the world
just as I do not belong to the world."*
JOHN 17:16

Lord, You made the sun and the planets and the
stars, but when You say that Your followers are not
of this world, I don't think You mean we're from
somewhere in outer space. We're a different kind
of alien. Lord, something inside me tells me how
wrong things are in this world. This is a planet
where things break down. You tell me that my true
home is with You, but I won't get there until either
I die or You bring us at the end times. In that new
earth, things won't break down. Not the mansions
that You are preparing for us, and especially not
the relationships. Thank You for making me a new
home.

Think about it:

As great as this world is, what do you think
the next one will be like? What does it
mean to be an alien in this world?

RUNNING THE RACE

You know that only one person gets a crown for being in a race even if many people run. You must run so you will win the crown. Everyone who runs in a race does many things so his body will be strong. He does it to get a crown that will soon be worth nothing, but we work for a crown that will last forever. In the same way, I run straight for the place at the end of the race. I fight to win. I do not beat the air. I keep working over my body. I make it obey me.
1 CORINTHIANS 9:24–27

Lord, may I run hard today and not stumble. I pray that I'll follow the rules. When people watch me run, may they see that I'm running toward You. Thank You for being my prize.

Think about it:

How is the Christian life like a race? What are some ways that you can train for the Christian life?

BeiNG YOUNG

*Josiah was eight years old when he became king.
And he ruled thirty-one years in Jerusalem.
He did what was right in the eyes of the Lord, and
walked in the ways of his father David. He did
not turn aside to the right or to the left.*

2 CHRONICLES 34:1–2

Lord, I don't need to be old to do the right thing. Lord, I pray that no matter how young I am, I do what's right in Your sight. I pray that I will walk in Your ways. Keep me on the narrow path and don't let me turn away. Whether I am a king who is responsible for a whole nation or just a kid who is responsible for keeping my room clean, I pray that You would guide me and help me take care of my responsibilities well. Help me choose wisely today.

Think about it:

How do you know what is right in the
sight of the Lord? What does it mean
to stay on the narrow path?

POPULARITY

*"For what does a man have if he gets all
the world and loses or gives up his life?"*
LUKE 9:25

Lord, I'm sure You know who the popular kids are. They dress cool, everyone wants to hang out with them, and whether or not they like someone can change how other kids treat that person. It is hard not to want to be part of the cool crowd, but You tell me that popularity doesn't matter to You. If I suddenly got popular or rich or powerful but didn't have You, none of it would matter. In fact, I know that if I'm living how You tell me to, I probably won't be popular. I pray that Your love for me will always be more important than what the cool kids think.

Think about it:

If you could be part of the cool crowd
if you'd stop praying, would you do it?
Why do other people's opinions matter so
much? How do you think God sees you?

OVERCOMING DOUBT

*At once Jesus put out His hand and took
hold of him. Jesus said to Peter, "You have
so little faith! Why did you doubt?"*
MATTHEW 14:31

Lord, there are times when I don't know if I believe all the things I've heard about You. If You are all-powerful, can You really be all good? Do You really hear me when I pray? Some people say You are not there at all. Lord, I pray that when doubt creeps into my mind, You reach out Your hand and take hold of me. Lord, even a little faith in You is more powerful than a lot of faith in the wrong thing. Help me believe the truth and live it out, not only so that I can see it, but so others will see it and believe in You too.

Think about it:

When you have doubts, do you talk to
God about them? What are the things
you know to be true about God?

70

STARTING NEW THINGS WITHOUT FINISHING OLD THINGS

The end of something is better than its beginning. Not giving up in spirit is better than being proud in spirit.
ECCLESIASTES 7:8

Lord, I like to start new things. There's something beautiful about the beginning of a project. But You tell me that finishing something I've started is better than starting new things. Lord, may I see the projects I start through to the end. Instead of proudly thinking I can do a lot of things well at the same time, teach me to patiently finish one project before moving on to another. Remind me that You delight in a job well done when it is done for You. Help me become a finisher and to not get frustrated when a project takes longer than I would like. Thank You for seeing me through to the end.

Think about it:

Do you ever start new things without finishing the old ones? What are some good things about finishing what you've started?

BRAVERY

*For God did not give us a spirit of fear. He gave us
a spirit of power and of love and of a good mind.*
2 TIMOTHY 1:7

Lord, when I am afraid, help me remember that
Your Spirit lives inside me. Nothing scares You, so
nothing needs to scare me either. Lord, You have
the power to change things to make them less
scary, but You also have the power to help me be
brave when nothing changes. Lord, help me think
clearly when fear makes things fuzzy. Thank
You for giving me Your Spirit. May I live in Your
power, love with Your strength, and think with Your
mind today and always. Lord, replace my fear with
Your love.

Think about it:

What kinds of things scare you? Knowing that
nothing scares God, and that He has given you
a spirit of power and love, how can you better
handle situations that frighten you?

RUMORS

"Do not tell a lie about someone else. Do not join with the sinful to say something that will hurt someone."
EXODUS 23:1

Father God, keep my lips from speaking lies about others, especially when I am angry at someone. When I think it would be funny to start a rumor about someone, help me think again. It takes a person a long time to build a good reputation, but that reputation can be ruined in a very short time. Lord, help me respect others by being honest. I know that any lies I tell will eventually catch up to me and my own reputation could be ruined. When my friends tell me something I'm not sure is true, give me the boldness to find out from the source. May I treat others with the same kindness I would like to receive. May I only speak the truth with love.

Think about it:

Have you ever told a lie to get someone else in trouble? How would you feel if someone told a lie about you?

BEING LIGHT IN A DARK WORLD

"You are the light of the world. You cannot hide a city that is on a mountain. Men do not light a lamp and put it under a basket. They put it on a table so it gives light to all in the house. Let your light shine in front of men. Then they will see the good things you do and will honor your Father Who is in heaven."
MATTHEW 5:14–16

Creator God, when I became Your child, You changed me from a creature of darkness into a being of light. Lord, I know I can't make Your light myself. The best I can do is reflect it into this dark world. I pray that when I do good things in this world, others won't think more of me but will see Your light reflecting and then praise You.

Think about it:

When other people see the things you do,
do they see God's light reflected? How can you
shine some light into someone's life today?

GOD'S INJURED FOLLOWERS

The king said, "Is there not still someone of the family of Saul to whom I may show the kindness of God?" And Ziba said to the king, "There is still a son of Jonathan who cannot walk because of his feet."

2 SAMUEL 9:3

Lord, You are the God of injured followers. Our injuries aren't always obvious. Some people need wheelchairs or are missing limbs, but others suffer depression or anxiety disorders. And yet, as injured as we are, You love us and want to show us kindness. Lord, never allow me to look down on those whose difficulties are different from my own. May I find ways to show Your kindness to anyone who needs it. Give me a compassionate heart like Yours. Help me not to stare but to simply see the person behind the injuries.

Think about it:

Do you know someone with a disability or injury who could use some help? What are some ways that you can show kindness and love to someone in need?

SEEMS RIGHT TO ME

There is a way which looks right to a man,
but its end is the way of death.
PROVERBS 14:12

Lord, I admit that I don't always have the best judgment. When I do things I want to do, sometimes I end up hurting myself or others. There are also things I know I should do, but they just don't sound like fun to me. When I trust my gut instead of listening for Your Spirit inside me, I get myself in trouble. Lord, help me listen to the right thing. Help me seek out what You want for me instead of what seems right to me. As I get better at listening, give me more of a desire to do what is right in Your eyes.

Think about it:

What are some things that seem good to you but you know are wrong? How can you listen more to what God wants for you than to what you want for yourself?

FAMILY HARMONY

See, how good and how pleasing it is
for brothers to live together as one!
PSALM 133:1

Father God, it would be nice if my family life were all peace and harmony, but it isn't. Sometimes, I argue with members of my family. It isn't always my fault, but sometimes it is. There are times when I feel like I don't belong in this family because I'm so different. Lord, I pray for some family harmony. I pray that the differences within my family would only make us stronger and help us live together in harmony. Lord, help me love my family and not pick fights. When I am in the wrong, help me admit it quickly so we can move on. When someone else is wrong, help me forgive just as quickly.

Think about it:

Do you ever feel like you don't fit with your family because you are so different? What can you do to live in harmony with your family, despite the differences?

PRETENDING HAS A DARK SIDE

*It is no surprise! The devil makes
himself look like an angel of light.*
2 CORINTHIANS 11:14

Lord, when I was younger, I would pretend while I played. I would pretend to be different superheroes or a character in an action movie. But pretending has a dark side too. Some people pretend things in order to get what they want. Some pretend they are sick in order to get medicine they don't need. Others pretend that someone hurt them in order to get another person in trouble. Lord, I pray that I would never pretend to be something I'm not in order to get what I want. Thank You for being real with me, for not just pretending to love me but *really* loving me. Let me never pretend with You or with anyone else You've put in my life.

Think about it:

Do you ever try to trick people by acting
in some way just to get what you want? How
would you feel if someone pretended with you?

NO EXPECTATIONS

But God had so much loving-kindness. He loved us with such a great love. Even when we were dead because of our sins, He made us alive by what Christ did for us. You have been saved from the punishment of sin by His loving-favor.
EPHESIANS 2:4–5

Lord, I know I don't deserve Your love, but You give it anyway. I didn't earn it by doing good things. You love me because it's part of who You are. Thank You for loving me. Lord, may I love like You do. May I love people, even when nothing about them makes me want to love them. Help me also to forgive like You do. Lord, You don't put conditions or expectations on Your love for me. I pray that I would be as free and generous with my love today.

Think about it:

When you love someone, is it because of what you'll get out of it? Can you forgive someone even before that person asks for it?

SOMETIMES, HEALING TAKES TIME

He took the blind man by the hand out of town.
Then He spit on the eyes of the blind man and put
His hands on him. He asked, "Do you see anything?"
The blind man looked up and said, "I see some men.
They look like trees, walking." Jesus put His hands
on the man's eyes again and told him to look up.
Then he was healed and saw everything well.
MARK 8:23–25

Lord, You can do anything You want. You healed a blind man by laying Your hands on him twice, because after the first time he could only see blurry images. I don't understand why You choose to heal some people instantly, why other people take time to heal, or why some people never get healed. But You are in charge, Lord. Help me simply trust Your wisdom.

Think about it:

Do you ever struggle with the fact that God heals some people but not others? Have you talked to God about these struggles?

DEATH AND RESURRECTION

Jesus said to her, "I am the One Who raises the dead and gives them life. Anyone who puts his trust in Me will live again, even if he dies."
JOHN 11:25

Lord Jesus, You are more powerful than everything, even death. It isn't that death is meaningless to You. Your death made it possible for me to have a relationship with God. But You didn't stop when You died. You came back to life and promised a second life for us as well. Lord, I believe that You lived and I believe that You died for my sins to pay the debt that I could not. I believe that You rose again from death. Lord, help me live in Your power and be an example of Your love today.

Think about it:

Do you ever worry about what happens after death? Do you believe that Jesus died for your sins? How can you live out your beliefs today so that other people notice God in you?

HUNGERING FOR RIGHTEOUSNESS

"Those who are hungry and thirsty to be right with God are happy, because they will be filled."
MATTHEW 5:6

Generous God, I am hungry almost all the time. It doesn't seem to matter if I ate less than an hour ago. If there's pizza or burgers or just food available, I'm hungry for it. Lord, may I be as hungry for doing the right things as I am for pizza. I pray that You will satisfy my needs and help me be hungry for the things You have for me. Lord, I would be grossed out if I were presented with spoiled meat. In the same way, may I turn up my nose at each opportunity to act selfishly. Give me a hunger for You, because I know You are happy to fill me.

Think about it:

Do you hunger for God's presence as much as you do for food? Is doing the wrong thing in God's eyes as gross to you as spoiled meat?

CONTENTMENT

*I am not saying I need anything. I have
learned to be happy with whatever I have.*
PHILIPPIANS 4:11

Lord, thank You for blessing me with the things I have. Help me not be greedy or disappointed because of the things I don't have. Thank You for the relationships You have brought into my life. Help me never take them for granted or treat people like they owe me something. Lord, thank You for the food I eat. Even when I'm hungry, I know I won't starve. I pray that I will learn to be as happy in the tough times as I am in the easy ones. I know that whether I am rich or poor, popular or friendless, full or hungry, You have already given me more than I deserve by loving me and calling me Your child.

Think about it:

Do you ever forget your blessings and instead focus on stuff you don't have? How can you become more content with what you do have?

BeING THe CLASS CLOWN

*A young man makes himself known by his
actions and proves if his ways are pure and right.*
PROVERBS 20:11

Lord, sometimes it is nice to be the center of attention. I like making people laugh. I like it when people know my name. Lord, I pray that people would know my name for good reasons, and not because I'm making a fool of myself. It can be fun to be a class clown, but I would rather be known for being trustworthy and respectful. If the way I act doesn't match the words I speak, I pray that You will correct me. Lord, help me act in a way You would approve of and remind me not to constantly try to win my friends' approval. I know that You, not I, should be the center of attention.

Think about it:

Do you enjoy making people smile? Do you ever take things too far because you like the attention? How can you make God the center of attention instead?

MODERN IDOLS

They served their gods,
which became a trap to them.
PSALM 106:36

Almighty God, only You have the power to save. But there are a lot of things around me that have the power to distract. Technology and hobbies and friends can all be good things, but when I focus more on them than I do on You, they become a kind of idol. Lord, help me keep You as my top focus. May my words be Your words. May I love with Your love. And may I act according to Your will. I pray that the good things in life don't become idols, leading to my downfall. I pray that no matter how much I like something, I would never worship it. Keep my priorities straight.

Think about it:

Do you have any modern idols distracting you from God? How can you keep your priorities where they should be?

SCRIPTURE MEMORIZATION

*Your Word have I hid in my heart,
that I may not sin against You.*
PSALM 119:11

Lord, You spoke all of creation into being. Then to make sure we knew it was Your work, You gave the right words to faithful men who wrote every book in the Bible. Thank You for introducing Yourself and giving me the words by which I can live well. Lord, give me a love for the Bible. It is far more special than any other book. May I remember the words inside and may they come to mind whenever I need them. I pray that I don't just remember the words, but that I would understand and apply them as well. May I be a living example of Your Word. Keep me from being a poor example or from using Your words for my own benefit instead of Yours.

Think about it:

How can memorizing God's Word keep you from sin? Does sin ever keep you from God's Word?

GeTTING ReVeNGe

Do not say, "I will punish wrong-doing."
Wait on the Lord, and He will take care of it.
PROVERBS 20:22

Lord, when someone does or says something un-kind to me, my first instinct is to take matters into my own hands and punish that person for how they treated me. But You tell me to wait for You to handle the matter. Even though waiting for justice is hard, I know that You can do things better than I can. Lord, help me wait patiently. Help me trust in Your timing and Your ways, even if it means I don't get to see the justice You have in mind. I pray that I don't dwell on what happened to me. And Lord, help me forgive, even when I don't feel like it.

Think about it:

Who do you think is better at giving justice,
you or God? What are some things you
can do to keep from reacting right away
to hurts others cause you?

PRAISING GOD FOR NATURE

The heavens are telling of the greatness of God and the great open spaces above show the work of His hands.
PSALM 19:1

Lord, Your creation is amazing. I can look at the night sky and see stars from horizon to horizon. You gave us constellations and made it possible for people to find their way around the world using nothing but the stars. You made the sun to give us warmth and light, which helps the plants grow so we have food and breathable air. You made the moon to reflect the light of the sun and to give us tides and help us number our days and months. Just by looking up, I can see that You are a God of order, that You are a generous Provider, and that You give light even in the darkest times. Thank You!

Think about it:

When was the last time you looked at the skies and thanked God for creation? What other things in nature are you thankful for today?

STRESS AND REST

"Come to Me, all of you who work and have heavy loads. I will give you rest."
MATTHEW 11:28

Jesus, it's easy for some grown-ups to think that because we don't have jobs, kids have it easy, but there are a lot of pressures on kids today. Between schoolwork and sports and the drama that goes along with friendships, there are times when I get stressed out. You know the pressures I feel, not only because You know everything, but also because You've experienced them for Yourself. You didn't just have responsibilities to Your earthly parents. You were responsible to Your heavenly Father as well. On top of that, You took the responsibility for the whole world's sin. Still, You promise to give me rest. Lord, thank You for being there when things get stressful. Help me find rest in You.

Think about it:

Do things going on in your life ever make you feel stressed? How can you leave those things in God's hands and get some rest?

SPECIAL PURPOSE

If a man lives a clean life, he will be like a dish made of gold. He will be respected and set apart for good use by the owner of the house.
2 TIMOTHY 2:21

Lord and Master, clean me up so I can be useful. If I needed some water, I wouldn't pick a dirty cup to put it in. I would look for a clean cup, ready to be used. You want me to be clean and ready too. I know You have created me for a special purpose. It isn't that You can't do good works without me, but You enjoy sharing the opportunity to show love to others. Lord, I pray that I would stay set apart for Your use, not dirtying myself with bad things, but ready and wanting to do good works for You.

Think about it:

What special purpose do you think God made you for? How can you make sure you are ready to accomplish that purpose when the chance comes along?

CONFESSING SINS

*If we tell Him our sins, He is faithful and we
can depend on Him to forgive us of our sins.
He will make our lives clean from all sin.*
1 JOHN 1:9

Lord, I was selfish again. I did what I wanted to instead of what You wanted for me. I'm sorry for sinning against You. Thank You for loving me and for promising to forgive me. I need it. I need You. I don't deserve Your forgiveness and there's nothing I could do to earn it, but that doesn't stop You from giving me grace over and over again. Lord, help me be faithful and righteous like You are. May I desire to do the right thing instead of the selfish thing. Thank You for loving me and for forgiving me.

Think about it:

Are there sins in your life that you should
talk to God about today? How do you think
confessing your sins might help you choose
better the next time you are tempted to sin?

CHOOSING FRIENDS

*Do not let anyone fool you. Bad people can
make those who want to live good become bad.*
1 CORINTHIANS 15:33

Lord, I need good friends. I pray that You would bring the right people into my life at the right times. Surround me with people who encourage me to do the right things. Lord, if there are people in my life who could influence me to do bad things, I pray that I'd have the strength to resist. If I can't stop myself when a person tempts me to do bad things, maybe it would be best not to see that person anymore. I pray that I will be true to You and that I'll be ready for every good work You've prepared for me. Thank You for being the ultimate Friend to me.

Think about it:

Do your friends encourage you to do good things or bad things? Do you encourage your friends to do good things? How do you think other people see your character?

PURITY

God wants you to be holy.
You must keep away from sex sins.
1 THESSALONIANS 4:3

All-seeing God, You know where my eyes look. You know what goes on in my mind. You know when I am tempted to look at things or think on things I shouldn't. Lord, I want to be holy like You are holy. You have set me aside for a special purpose, and when I treat people like they are there for my pleasure, I can't accomplish that purpose. You made all people in Your image, and my desires themselves aren't evil. But You provided marriage as a way to fulfill those desires. I just need some patience. Lord, give me the strength I need to stay pure for the person You have for me. Make me holy.

Think about it:

Are you tempted to look at things or think about things that you shouldn't? How can you change your routines and surroundings to help you fight those temptations?

LYING

Do not lie to each other. You have put out of your life your old ways. You have now become a new person and are always learning more about Christ. You are being made more like Christ. He is the One Who made you.
COLOSSIANS 3:9–10

Lord, when I accepted Your gift of salvation, You gave me a new mind that desires You. But even though You made me new, the old habits and desires still bother me. Lord, help me to always be honest. Whether I'm tempted to get someone else in trouble by telling lies, or whether I'm trying to avoid getting in trouble myself, I pray that I always stick to the truth. Help me embrace the new person You've made me to be. Help me to be a person who always tells the truth, even when it costs me.

Think about it:

In what kinds of situations might you be tempted to speak untruthfully? Why do you think telling the truth is the best thing to do, even when it is uncomfortable?

GOD'S WILL FOR YOUR LIFE

Be full of joy all the time. Never stop praying.
In everything give thanks. This is what God
wants you to do because of Christ Jesus.
1 THESSALONIANS 5:16–18

Lord, sometimes I worry about what I'm supposed to do in life. But You've already given me some directions to follow. I may not have control over the things that happen to me, but You gave me control over my attitude. Help me choose joy. You may not tell me every decision I should make, but You want me to pray and talk to You about my life. Remind me to pray often. I may not know specifically what job I'll have when I grow up, but I know I should be thankful for the things I can do now. Lord, when I worry about the future, remind me of what I can do now.

Think about it:

Do you ever worry about God's will for your life? What do you think He wants you doing right now?

PERSISTENCE

*Even very young men get tired and become weak
and strong young men trip and fall. But they who
wait upon the Lord will get new strength. They will
rise up with wings like eagles. They will run and not
get tired. They will walk and not become weak.*
ISAIAH 40:30–31

Lord, when I am tired and feeling weak, I need You.
When I am strong and feeling confident, I still
need You. I can't handle the wild winds of life on
my own. But You know the winds and can use them
to help me fly like an eagle. You invite me to use
Your strength as I go through this life. Lord, be my
strength. May I keep on the tasks You have set before me, using the strength only You can provide.

Think about it:

When you are feeling strong, do you ever feel
like you don't need God's help? How can you
make sure you're relying on God's strength all
the time, not just when you are feeling weak?

LOVING IN WORD AND DEED

If a person says, "I love God," but hates his brother, he is a liar. If a person does not love his brother whom he has seen, how can he love God Whom he has not seen?
1 JOHN 4:20

Lord, it is one thing for me to say something and another thing to do it. Love is one of the easiest things in the world to say. I couldn't count the times in a week that I say that I love something. I love pizza. I love a TV show. I love my family. Sometimes, I even say I love something when I don't, just to make someone happy. Lord, keep me from lying about love. May my actions and attitudes give that word special meaning. Above all, may my love for You be true.

Think about it:

Do you ever say you love something when you really don't? Do your actions and words match when you say you love someone?

WHY SHOULD I FORGIVE?

"If you forgive people their sins, your Father in heaven will forgive your sins also. If you do not forgive people their sins, your Father will not forgive your sins."
MATTHEW 6:14–15

Forgiving God, there have been tons of times when I have needed Your forgiveness, and You gave it to me every time. I know You always forgive people when they confess their sin, but it isn't always easy for me to forgive. When someone does something mean to me, I want to get even. But since I'm Your child, it isn't my job or my right to do so. Lord, help me forgive people when they hurt me. Help me show them that I'm really Your follower. When forgiveness comes hard to me, remind me what it cost You to forgive me.

Think about it:

What would it say about you as a follower of Christ that He forgave you, but you can't forgive someone else? Why is forgiveness so important?

FAITHFUL OVER A LITTLE

"His owner said to him, 'You have done well. You are a good and faithful servant. You have been faithful over a few things. I will put many things in your care. Come and share my joy.'"
MATTHEW 25:23

Lord, help me take care of my chores well. I may not have a lot of responsibilities right now, but that doesn't mean I can take it easy. I know that when I am faithful in the things I need to do now, I'll get more responsibilities later. Lord, help me grow up to be capable for the tasks ahead. If I'm tempted to slack off, remind me that I'm actually working for You, even when my parents or teachers assign the work to me. When the tasks get tough, help me to stay with them until they are finished, working carefully to do a good job.

Think about it:

Do you carefully finish the chores
and jobs you have right now? Do you
always do your best work on them?

THE FRUIT OF THE SPIRIT

*But the fruit that comes from having the Holy
Spirit in our lives is: love, joy, peace, not giving up,
being kind, being good, having faith, being gentle,
and being the boss over our own desires.*
GALATIANS 5:22–23

Lord, I need Your Holy Spirit's help to be the kind of person You want me to be. Let me love like You. Give me joy when I am sad. Give me peace when I am stressed. Lord, help me always finish the task at hand. May I answer mean words with kind ones. May I obey the rules when I would rather do my own thing. Lord, give me faith when I face doubt. Give me gentleness when I would rather kick and scream. Help me overcome my selfish wants. I can only do these things with the help of Your Holy Spirit.

Think about it:

What evidence is there that the Holy Spirit lives inside you? Do you think other people can notice the fruits of the Holy Spirit in you?

Whenever You Need God

Let us go with complete trust to the throne of God.
We will receive His loving-kindness and have
His loving-favor to help us whenever we need it.
HEBREWS 4:16

Lord, I don't know why You choose to love me. I don't have to be afraid of You or how You'll respond when I ask for Your help. I'll never be so dirty that You won't hug me. I don't have to try to clean up my mess before I come to You. Lord, when I feel like hiding, when I feel like putting things off because I'm afraid of how they'll turn out, give me the boldness I need to come to You. Help me trust in what You've said. Thank You for loving me and for always being there for me.

Think about it:

Do you ever feel like running away when you should actually be running toward God? What does God say when you are afraid He won't love you?

GIRL TROUBLES

Do not desire her beauty in your heart.
Do not let her catch you with her eyes.
PROVERBS 6:25

Lord, I know that You said back in the garden of Eden that it wasn't good for the man to be alone. That's why You made a woman. But sometimes, girls can be a major distraction. Lord, I pray that my mind will stay focused, that my eyes will stay clean, and that my actions will be pure. Don't let me get pulled into a bad situation because of a girl, no matter how good she looks. It isn't that girls are bad. They bear Your image every bit as much as boys. But there will be time to focus on girls later in life. May I become more like You so I can be the right kind of man when that time comes.

Think about it:

Are you ever tempted to act differently
around girls you like? What can you do
now to be the best guy for a girl later in life?

MOVING MOUNTAINS

Jesus said to them, "For sure, I tell you this: If you
have faith and do not doubt, you will not only be able
to do what was done to the fig tree. You will also be
able to say to this mountain, 'Move from here and be
thrown into the sea,' and it will be done. All things you
ask for in prayer, you will receive if you have faith."
MATTHEW 21:21–22

Glorious God, You are powerful beyond imagination. You tell me that Your power is available to me. I think You enjoy using Your power for my good when it brings You glory. Lord, I want a vibrant prayer life and a faith that does not fail. May I make my requests with the right motivation, and may they be answered in ways that clearly show Your involvement. Move mountains, Lord, and take the glory.

Think about it:

Do you think God enjoys stretching His muscles for your requests? What "mountains" in your life do you want God to move for you?

MAKE THE MOST OF YOUR TIME

So be careful how you live. Live as men who are wise and not foolish. Make the best use of your time. These are sinful days. Do not be foolish. Understand what the Lord wants you to do.
EPHESIANS 5:15–17

Lord, there are only so many hours in a day but so many things I want to do. Help me make the most of my time. If there's something You have planned for me that isn't on my to-do list, help me recognize it and do it well. May I not make foolish choices when there are so many options calling for my attention. Lord, I pray that Your will would be my top priority, today and every day. Help me appreciate the time I have here on earth.

Think about it:

Do you believe you use your time wisely? Do you make time to spend with God each day? How can you use some time today to take care of someone else's needs?

BEING KNOWN AS A CHRISTIAN

"I give you a new Law. You are to love each other. You must love each other as I have loved you. If you love each other, all men will know you are My followers."
JOHN 13:34–35

Lord Jesus, I was born into a family and I have a family name. I know that Christ wasn't Your last name. You are the Savior of the world and Christ is the title You hold. You saved me because You love me, and You call me to love like You do. I became part of Your family when I accepted Your gift of salvation. I pray that in the same way people know I'm a member of my earthly family because I share their last name, people will know that I'm part of Your family because I share Your love with them.

Think about it:

What does it mean to be part of God's family? Do you think people know you are a Christian by your love for others?

MAKING THE SAME MISTAKE OVER AND OVER AGAIN

A fool who does his foolish act again is like a
dog that turns back to what he has thrown up.
PROVERBS 26:11

Perfect God, You don't make mistakes, but I do. I know You love me, even when I make mistakes. But we both wish I wouldn't make so many. Lord, forgive me when I mess up, and help me to learn from my mistakes and not repeat them. It's a gross thing when a dog throws up, but even grosser when it goes back and eats it again. The dog probably shouldn't have eaten the thing that made it throw up in the first place, but it may have looked good at the time. Help me be wiser than the dog. May I see the sins I'm tempted to repeat as unappetizing as dog vomit.

Think about it:

What do you do when you make a mistake?
How can you avoid that mistake in the future?

SPEAKING UP WHEN SOMETHING ISN'T RIGHT

"If your brother sins against you, go and tell him
what he did without other people hearing it. If
he listens to you, you have won your brother back
again. But if he will not listen to you, take one
or two other people with you. Every word may be
remembered by the two or three who heard."
MATTHEW 18:15–16

Father God, You know what it is like when someone is against You. When my friends do something
mean to me, it is tempting to act like nothing happened, but that doesn't fix anything. It's good to
forgive, but if someone has hurt me, my relationship with them gets hurt too. Give me the boldness
I need to talk to my friends when I'm hurt. Lord,
You know how to heal relationships. Please heal the
ones between my friends and me.

Think about it:

How do you respond when one of your
friends hurts you? What steps can you
take to heal the relationship?

STAY AWAKE

"Watch and pray so that you will not be tempted. Man's spirit is willing, but the body does not have the power to do it."
MATTHEW 26:41

Lord, You said the words in the verse above when You wanted Your disciples to wait with You the night You were betrayed. They let You down. They fell asleep as they waited. Under my own power, I would have fallen asleep too. I want to do what is right, but I can't do it on my own. I need Your power inside me to help me stay close to You. Lord, may I stay awake in my duties. Thinking I can do it alone is just the first step to failure. Lord, help me to watch and pray and not grow tired.

Think about it:

Do you ever feel like you can do something on your own, only to find out you don't have the strength? What are you doing to bring Jesus into the situation to help you stay awake?

RICHES

*"Do not gather together for yourself riches of this earth.
They will be eaten by bugs and become rusted. Men
can break in and steal them. Gather together riches in
heaven where they will not be eaten by bugs or become
rusted. Men cannot break in and steal them. For wherever
your riches are, your heart will be there also."*
MATTHEW 6:19–21

Lord, may I value what You value. While others day-dream about winning the lottery, let me work on bringing You glory. If I were to suddenly become rich, I know that I'd be tempted to use the money on myself instead of sharing it with those in need. But I also know that if I shared it with others, I would be rewarded in heaven. Lord, help me see beyond this life and focus on what matters to You in the long run.

Think about it:

How important is money to you? How can
you use what you have to bring God glory?

THE CROWN OF LIFE

The man who does not give up when tests come is happy. After the test is over, he will receive the crown of life. God has promised this to those who love Him.
JAMES 1:12

Lord, when I'm having a hard day, I just want to go to my room and hide. But You tell me that I'll be happier if I finish a hard day well. In fact, You tell me that when I have made it through a difficult time, I'll get the crown of life. Hard days aren't fun, but it is good to have a reward to look forward to when I'm having one. Lord, help me face difficult times with a good attitude. Help me not give up. Thank You for Your promises and Your love. Thank You for the crown of life.

Think about it:

How would not giving up when things get tough make you a happy person? How would remembering God's rewards help you get through a hard day?

LOVING THE POOR

He who hates his neighbor sins, but happy
is he who shows loving-favor to the poor.
PROVERBS 14:21

Father God, You made the world. It is all Yours—
all the money, all the stuff, all of everything. But it
is easy to forget that when I see people with more
than me. And it is easy to forget that everything
is Yours when I see people with less than me too.
Then, I can feel guilty about the stuff I do have.
But You tell me I'll be happy if I am kind to people
who don't have much. Give me a heart for the poor.
Since everything belongs to You, I don't really own
anything more than a poor person anyway. Lord,
thank You for providing for my needs. Help me
provide for others.

Think about it:

What do you think it means to show "loving-favor"
to the poor? Why does the amount of money
someone has make them liked or disliked?

FALLING SHORT

*For all men have sinned and have
missed the shining-greatness of God.*
ROMANS 3:23

Lord, I don't think I'm a bad kid. I try hard most of
the time. I don't usually go looking for trouble. And
I know at least a handful of kids who are worse than
me. But it doesn't matter how good or bad I am in
Your eyes, because I am not perfect. Only You are
perfect. Whenever I am selfish or mean or jealous, I
prove the fact that I'm not perfect. Lord, thank You
for loving me and saving me in spite of the fact that
I fall short of perfection. Thank You for being perfect, since only Your perfect sacrifice on the cross
could reconnect me with You. Help me live in Your
grace and be more like You.

Think about it:

Have you heard people say that as long as
the good stuff they do outweighs the bad,
then God will let them into heaven? What
does the verse above say about that?

PRIDE BEFORE THE FALL

When pride comes, then comes shame,
but wisdom is with those who have no pride.
PROVERBS 11:2

Lord, keep me humble. When I start showing off, I get into trouble. If I didn't act like I was better at something than I am, I wouldn't embarrass myself when asked to prove it. It is tempting to be prideful. I want people to like me and to think I'm cool. Lord, help me realize that the coolest thing I can do is to be genuine. When I don't put on an act, I can truly be myself and people can like me for who I am instead of who I pretend to be. Thank You for making me unique. Help me embrace myself and not take pride in things I can't do. May others see me for me.

Think about it:

Do you ever brag about your abilities?
Which is better: when someone else tells
you that you do something well, or when
you tell others that you do something well?

MARCHING ORDERS

"Go and make followers of all the nations. Baptize them in the name of the Father and of the Son and of the Holy Spirit. Teach them to do all the things I have told you. And I am with you always, even to the end of the world."
MATTHEW 28:19–20

Lord, before You went back to heaven, You gave us some jobs to do while we wait for You to come back. Give me boldness so I can tell people about You and Your love for them. Make my life an advertisement for Christianity. I pray that others will see that You are with me. Thank You for inviting me into Your family. I pray that You give me the words to say and things to do that will bring other people into that family. May I follow Your marching orders until You come back for me.

Think about it:

Have you talked to any of your friends
about Jesus? Do they know that
you are part of His family?

PLANNING AHEAD

*"If one of you wanted to build a large building, you
would sit down first and think of how much money it
would take to build it. You would see if you had enough
money to finish it, or when the base of the building is
finished, you might see that you do not have enough
money to finish it. Then all who would see it would
make fun of you. They would say, 'This man began
to build and was not able to finish.'"*

LUKE 14:28–30

Lord, help me plan ahead. Give me the patience it
takes to make a plan, even if I really want to get
started without one. Lord, I pray that You would
bring the right people into my life to help each
project succeed, even if they challenge how I want
to do it.

Think about it:

Do you ever start projects without first thinking
them through? What can you do to make sure
your idea is fully developed before you start?

FORGIVE YOUR SIBLINGS

Try to understand other people. Forgive each
other. If you have something against someone,
forgive him. That is the way the Lord forgave you.
COLOSSIANS 3:13

Lord, why do siblings have to cause such trouble? Sometimes it feels like our parents are the only things we have in common. It's hard to understand them and why they bother me so much. I need Your help to understand. I need Your help to forgive. It shouldn't matter what my brother or sister has done to me, but it is difficult to let go of things. But that's exactly what You did. I didn't deserve Your forgiveness, but You gave it to me. Lord, help me forgive like that, even before my siblings ask for it. Help me see things from their perspective.

Think about it:

When was the last time you fought with a sibling or close friend? Can you understand their side of the argument? Have you forgiven them and asked them to make things right with you?

LOSING LOVED ONES

*"Those who have sorrow are happy,
because they will be comforted."*
MATTHEW 5:4

Lord, I don't understand right now how I'm supposed to be happy. I'm sad that I've lost someone close to me. It feels like there's a hole in my life. I need You to fill that hole. I need the comfort You promise those who are sad. I don't understand why You chose to take my loved one away from me, but You must have a plan I can't see. Help me trust in Your plan. It will take time to heal from this, but I know that You will stand by my side, even when I don't see You, even when I'm upset with You because I'm going through this.

Think about it:

Have you ever been angry with God for
allowing the loss of someone special to you?
Did you talk to God about it? Did you talk with
your parents about how you were feeling?

GOD'S SPIRIT

*He has given us His Spirit. This is how
we live by His help and He lives in us.*
1 JOHN 4:13

Father God, You made the world and everything
in it. Nothing happens that You don't know about.
Lord Jesus, You saved the world from sin. Nothing
happens that You didn't save us from. Holy Spirit,
You live inside of me. Nothing happens that You
don't care about. When I pray, the Holy Spirit in
me talks to the Father because Jesus has made it
possible. Lord, it amazes me that You involve me
in what could be a private conversation with Yourself. Thank You for loving me and for giving me
the Holy Spirit. Thank You for the Son's sacrifice.
Thank You for making me. Help me listen to the
Spirit's guidance. May I always do what You would
have me do.

Think about it:

What does it mean to you to have the Holy
Spirit living inside you? Do you listen
when the Holy Spirit is prompting you?

IRON SHARPENS IRON

Iron is made sharp with iron,
and one man is made sharp by a friend.
PROVERBS 27:17

Loving God, thank You for my friends. I pray that I would be a good friend in both easy times and tough ones. Sometimes the sharpening process is painful, but I depend on the honesty of my friends to help me be a better person. When my friends are doing things I think are wrong, give me the boldness to speak up to them. Even good friends fight about stuff, but I pray that any arguments I have with my friends would be short-lived. I believe that just like a sharp sword is more useful than a dull one, a good friendship is useful to You and what You have planned for me. May my friends and I be ready and eager to serve You.

Think about it:

How can you help your friends become better people? How can they do that for you?

FAITH IN AN UNSEEN GOD

You have never seen Him but you love Him. You cannot see Him now but you are putting your trust in Him. And you have joy so great that words cannot tell about it. You will get what your faith is looking for, which is to be saved from the punishment of sin.
1 PETER 1:8–9

Unseen God, open my eyes to see Your love for me. Open my heart to love You in return. Open my mind to believe in You and trust You more every day. I can't see You, but I know You are real and that You love me. I don't need to see air to breathe or gravity to stay stuck to the ground. You are like life-giving air and like gravity in that I can allow You to control my every action. You are real, and I have faith in You.

Think about it:

What are some things you can't see
but know are there? You can't see God,
so how do you know He's there for you?

DON'T WORRY, BE PRAYERFUL

Do not worry. Learn to pray about everything. Give thanks to God as you ask Him for what you need.
PHILIPPIANS 4:6

Powerful God, nothing is out of Your control, but I sometimes forget that. So many things could happen that I have no control over. Natural disasters could destroy my home, the people I love could move away or get sick, and people with bad intentions could hurt me or my friends. But I don't need to worry about these things because You are still in control of the world. You never promised that bad things won't happen, only that You'll be there for me when they do. Lord, help me focus on the blessings that come from You rather than the things I'm tempted to worry about.

Think about it:

What can keep you from worrying about things you can't control? What kinds of things should you pray about when you are worried? What are you thankful for today?

A GREATER LOVE

*"No one can have greater love than
to give his life for his friends."*
JOHN 15:13

Loving God, I'll probably never be in a situation where I have to die in place of my friends. But I have opportunities every day to sacrifice my wants and make someone else's day better. It could be something as simple as giving up my favorite place to sit for someone or something more serious, like sacrificing my time to help a friend who's struggling in a class at school. Either way, please give me the desire to show my friends real love. Lord, You are the ultimate example of self-sacrifice. Thank You for dying in my place, and thank You for living in me and helping me love others. May I have a chance today to lay down what I want for someone else.

Think about it:

What are some ways you can show love to your
friends today? When was the last time you
sacrificed something you wanted for someone else?

HOLY SPIRIT, GUIDANCE COUNSELOR

"The Helper is the Holy Spirit. The Father will send Him in My place. He will teach you everything and help you remember everything I have told you."
JOHN 14:26

Holy God, I may not understand how You can be one God but three different persons, but I am thankful for all three: the Father, the Son (Jesus), and the Holy Spirit. Father, thank You for being perfect and providing for me. Jesus, thank You for taking my punishment and making a way for me to be forgiven. Spirit, thank You for being my Guide. Thank You for guiding me to You and for giving me Your Spirit. May I listen to the Spirit's promptings to stay out of trouble and to be led toward the good works You have for me to do.

Think about it:

What does it mean to you that God lives inside of you in the form of the Holy Spirit? How can you listen better to His direction?

WATCH YOUR TALK

*Watch your talk! No bad words should be coming
from your mouth. Say what is good. Your words
should help others grow as Christians.*
EPHESIANS 4:29

Lord, may the words that come out of my mouth be honoring to You. Help me to resist the temptation to swear or use dirty language or tell lies. Help me not to join in when I'm with other guys and they use dirty language. Give me the right words to say to help others become better people. It may be something nice like a compliment, but sometimes it will be a gentle confrontation. In any case, help me choose my words carefully. Make my message match my life so that no one can question that I follow Jesus.

Think about it:

Do you ever swear when you get angry or when you want to make other people think you are cool?
If your words are the only thing people know about you, will they know that you are a Christian?

BULLIES

"I say to you who hear Me, love those who work against you. Do good to those who hate you. Respect and give thanks for those who try to bring bad to you. Pray for those who make it very hard for you."
LUKE 6:27–28

Lord, help me do the impossible by giving me the strength to resist mean thoughts toward bullies when they are mean to me. Help me to love them despite their actions. May I find ways to be kind when they are unkind. May I show respect when they are disrespectful to me. I pray that You would bless people who aren't nice to me. Surround them with people who love them, starting with me. Only You have the power to change hearts and minds, and I pray that You would change me, not those who bully me, first.

Think about it:

How do you feel when a bully is being mean to you? What are some nice things you could do for that person?

THE COOL STUFF

Keep your minds thinking about things in heaven.
Do not think about things on the earth.
COLOSSIANS 3:2

Lord, things change fast here on earth. What is cool one day is uncool the next. Technology makes it so that even if I did have the newest thing at one time, it would be old soon after. Movies and clothes and words all change from cool to old so quickly that it is hard to keep up. But You do not change. You don't want me chasing after the latest trend but after You. May I work more on making the world a better place by spreading Your love. Lord, change my perspective and make it like Yours. May I not be tempted when I see the cool stuff around me. Help me see what matters to You.

Think about it:

Why do you think you worry about being cool and having the newest stuff? How would things be different if you looked for opportunities to show love to others instead?

GOD OVER THE GOVERNMENT

"Show Me a piece of money." They brought Him a piece.
Jesus said to them, "Whose picture is this? Whose name
is on it?" They said to Him, "Caesar's." Then He said to
them, "Pay to Caesar the things that belong to Caesar.
Pay to God the things that belong to God."
MATTHEW 22:19–21

Holy God, when the Pharisees tried to trick Jesus into making a political statement, He turned it around on them. Whether we agree with government practices or who the leader is, we are first called to give You the respect You deserve. The government and everyone in it must give account to You in the end. Lord, may I stand up for the right things and not put my confidence in any person who isn't You. Give the leaders of this nation wisdom and help them follow You.

Think about it:

Do people you know get upset about the government? How can you know for sure that nothing happens that God doesn't allow?

HUMILITY

Everyone who is proud in heart is a shame to the Lord. For sure, that one will be punished.
PROVERBS 16:5

Lord, give me a humble heart. When I see myself as smarter or stronger or better than I really am, I open myself to being proved wrong. Whenever I think I don't need Your help or the help of people around me, I end up looking foolish when I can't do something by myself. Lord, save me from myself and my pride. I pray that I would have a good idea of the things I am capable of and that I'd be willing to ask for help with everything else. Help me never to feel like I can handle things better than You can. You are God. Never let me forget how much I need You.

Think about it:

Have you ever tried to do more than you can handle alone? Has your pride ever led to you failing to accomplish something?

FAITH IN ACTION

*My Christian brothers, what good does it do if you
say you have faith but do not do things that prove
you have faith? Can that kind of faith save you from
the punishment of sin? What if a Christian does not
have clothes or food? And one of you says to him,
"Goodbye, keep yourself warm and eat well." But if you
do not give him what he needs, how does that help him?
A faith that does not do things is a dead faith.*

JAMES 2:14–17

Lord, I want a faith that is alive. I want a faith that
is active. I want a faith that is real. I pray that I will
see others' needs and that I will be able to help.
I know that if I don't take care of people's needs,
they might see my faith in You as pointless.

Think about it:

Why is it important to God that you help
others who are in need? How can you best
help take care of people around you?

LIVING LIKE A NEW CREATION

*For if a man belongs to Christ, he is a new
person. The old life is gone. New life has begun.*
2 CORINTHIANS 5:17

Lord, help me live my life as the new creation the Bible says I am. I'm human and I make mistakes, but that is no excuse to give up and be okay with sin. You saved me from the bad choices I made before I came to know You. You also saved me from the bad choices I will make in the future. Lord, keep me from feeling like Your love and forgiveness is a permission slip to sin. Thank You for giving me a clean start every day. May I not repeat the mistakes I made in the past. May I be wise enough to avoid different ones in the future.

Think about it:

What do you think it looks like to live
like a new creation? Are you asking God
to help you to avoid bad choices now?

GOD LOVES YOU

We love Him because He loved us first.
1 JOHN 4:19

Almighty God, I sometimes can't believe You would love me. I'm far from perfect. I make silly mistakes and I'm more selfish than I should be. But You love me anyway. It should be easy for me to love You because You are perfect. But even though You are worthy of my love, sometimes I can't see past myself and my wants. Lord, help me love You with a pure heart. The only reason I can love You at all is because You loved me first. Thank You for loving me first so that I can love You in return. Help me love others like You love me, never thinking about my own needs but the needs of other people.

Think about it:

If God loves you even though you don't deserve it, how should you love other people? What things get in the way of you loving God right now? What can you do about them?

GUARD YOUR HEART

*Keep your heart pure for out of it
are the important things of life.*
PROVERBS 4:23

Lord, keep my heart pure. I pray that I wouldn't allow myself to get caught up in the wrong things. Keep my heart from loving things more than people. Keep my heart from loving people more than I love You. Keep me from getting attached to the wrong people at the wrong times. If I have a crush on someone, help me understand that the best thing I can do is treat her with respect and kindness, but never let her take Your place in my heart. If I give my heart to something or someone instead of loving You with all of my strength, I'll be missing out on the most important things in life.

Think about it:

Is your heart purely set on God, or is it divided
with people and things too? What are some
important things you could miss out on
by not keeping your heart pure?

BE STRONG

Be strong. Be strong in heart,
all you who hope in the Lord.
PSALM 31:24

Almighty God, help me to be strong. Although I think it would be great to be strong enough to lift a car over my head, I don't think physical strength is the most important kind of strength. May I have a strong faith in You, strong enough to enable me to overcome doubts when they come. May I have strong character so I can overcome temptations. May I have a strong resolve so I can overcome laziness when I just don't feel like doing the things I need to do. May I have a strong memory so I can recall Your Word when I need it most. Lord, thank You for being the source of my strength. Don't let me do the heavy lifting alone.

Think about it:

When you hear that someone is strong, what do you think of first? In what area do you need the Lord's strength most?

A SHARING ATTITUDE

*Nothing should be done because of pride
or thinking about yourself. Think of other
people as more important than yourself.*
PHILIPPIANS 2:3

Lord, I know I should treat other people as more important than me, but that isn't easy to do. When someone else has something that I want, I don't always feel like waiting for it. Instead, I feel like taking the thing for myself. Lord, stop me from being selfish. Help me focus less on myself and more on how I can take care of other people. May my wants never be at the expense of someone else's happiness. I know that it isn't bad for me to want things for myself, but help me learn the best timing and way to ask. And if I can share the thing I want, give me a sharing attitude.

Think about it:

Do you struggle when someone else has
something you want for yourself? How can
you make it a practice to think of others
before you think of yourself?

CHOOSING JOY

*They have been put to the test by much trouble,
but they have much joy. They have given
much even though they were very poor.*
2 CORINTHIANS 8:2

Lord, may my joy in life not depend on what I'm going through now, but on where I'm going to later. You never promised this life would be easy. I know I'm going to have troubles. I may never be rich here on earth. But You have promised that I will be with You after this life is done. Help me to see that any troubles I have here are temporary and any riches I have will pass. Let me serve You well through times of trouble and good times alike. Be my joy today.

Think about it:

What do you have to look forward to since
you have given your life to Christ? How
can you use your riches and talents for
others while you are here on earth?

LIGHT FOR THE PATH

*Your Word is a lamp to my feet
and a light to my path.*
PSALM 119:105

Lord, I need Your guidance. So many people tell me what I should do, where I should go, and how I should act. Sometimes I feel like I just want to do my own thing. But my own thing may not be the best thing. I need a reliable guide. Lord, help me look to You and to the Bible to find out how I should live and what I should do. You didn't give me the Bible so I would know what to eat for my next meal. You gave me the Bible so I could get to know You and how You think. Help me to think like You. Give me the directions I need to see and avoid problems on my path ahead.

Think about it:

How does the Bible give light to your path in life? What kinds of things does it say you should be doing right now?

GOOD NEWS WORTH SHARING

*I am not ashamed of the Good News. It is the
power of God. It is the way He saves men from the
punishment of their sins if they put their trust in Him.
It is for the Jew first and for all other people also.*
ROMANS 1:16

Lord Jesus, thank You for saving me. Calling the love You've shown me "Good News" is an understatement. I deserve to be punished for the selfish choices I make, but You took the punishment for me. Help me to keep trusting in You. May I be bold in sharing the message of Your love with my friends and family. You freely offer salvation to everyone who is willing to listen. I just need to be willing to tell people about You. Thank You for loving me enough to die in my place.

Think about it:

Who was the last person you told about what
Jesus is doing in your life? Who is one person
you think needs to hear about Jesus today?

REPUTATIONS

The honor of good people will lead them, but those who hurt others will be destroyed by their own false ways.
PROVERBS 11:3

Lord, I've heard that reputations take a lifetime to build and a few minutes to ruin. I want to have a good reputation. I pray that I will be an honorable person, that people will see me as trustworthy and well-behaved because I deserve those labels. Keep me from lying or trying to trick people. Keep me from being fake. I won't always do the right thing, but I pray that I wouldn't try to hide my mistakes. Help me apologize and try to make things right when I mess up. Help me to build up and protect my own reputation.

Think about it:

What do you want people to think of when your name comes up? Do you want them to think of your honesty and hard work, or your selfishness? What can you do to improve your reputation?

TESTS

My Christian brothers, you should be
happy when you have all kinds of tests.
JAMES 1:2

Lord, tests aren't usually fun. Whether I'm being tested on my science knowledge or in my gym class or in my personal life, I don't always enjoy tests. But You say that I should be happy when I'm tested. Lord, let the tests I face prove that I've been paying attention to the things I'm supposed to be learning. When I'm tested on my schoolwork, help me remember the things the teachers have taught me. When hard things happening in my life test me, help me remember that You are always faithful. Lord, may I prepare well for each test, knowing that You love me regardless of the outcome.

Think about it:

Do you always prepare the very best you can for each school test you take? How can you best prepare for the tests life throws at you?

ASKING INSTEAD OF FIGHTING

What starts wars and fights among you? Is it not because you want many things and are fighting to have them? You want something you do not have, so you kill. You want something but cannot get it, so you fight for it. You do not get things because you do not ask for them.

JAMES 4:1–2

Lord, I've heard it said that some things are worth fighting for. But fighting over things like toys and games and clothes probably doesn't count. It is tempting when someone has something I want to fight with them and take it. Even if I don't actually fight, that feeling is still there. Asking politely for things isn't always my first idea, but it should be. Lord, help me remember to ask when I want something. You love me and have promised to take care of my needs when I ask. Lord, help me ask for good things.

Think about it:

When you want something, do you ask politely for it? What is something worth asking politely for?

HIDING SINS VS. CONFESSING SINS

*It will not go well for the man who hides
his sins, but he who tells his sins and turns
from them will be given loving-pity.*
PROVERBS 28:13

Lord, when I sin, I just want to hide. I know I've done something wrong, and I don't want anyone to find out. What if they stop liking me? What if I get into trouble? But You invite me to tell You my sins and my struggles. You love me regardless of my sins. There will always be consequences for my actions, but as long as You love me, I can face them. I can't hide my sins from You, so help me be honest and open when it comes to mistakes I make. Forgive me and help me choose better in the future.

Think about it:

Are you hiding anything you should confess?
Why are you hiding these things? What keeps
you from admitting your sins and putting
them behind you right now?

COMPETITION

"Many who are first will be last.
Many who are last will be first."
MATTHEW 19:30

Lord, I want to be the best in everything I do. I want to run the fastest, work the hardest, and be the smartest. I want other people to look at me and think I'm special and amazing. And while it is good for me to work hard and try my best, what You think of me matters much more than what people around me think. When I compete with other people, help me not get lost in the competition. I want to do my best, but help me be happy for my competitors if they do better than me. If I start to think too highly of myself and my abilities, gently remind me that You don't judge me based on how fast or smart I am.

Think about it:

Does competition bring out the best in you or the worst? How do you treat the people who compete against you?

KINDNESS TO ANIMALS

A man who is right with God cares for his animal,
but the sinful man is hard and has no pity.
PROVERBS 12:10

Lord, thank You for making so many amazing, beautiful, mysterious, and sometimes dangerous animals. Whether it is wild or tame, a neighborhood cat or a pet dog, I pray that I would always treat animals with kindness. How I treat animals is important because it shows that I respect You and the things You have made. Help me do my part to take care of the creation You have entrusted to humanity. I pray that if I see someone being cruel to animals, I would have the boldness to say something. Thank You for making animals to be our companions. Help me be a good companion to the animals in my care and those I encounter in nature.

Think about it:

How do you think God feels about the animals He made? Who can you talk to when you see someone being mean to animals?

JeALOUSY

A heart that has peace is life to the body, but wrong desires are like the wasting away of the bones.
PROVERBS 14:30

Lord, give me peace when it comes to the things I want. I see my friends who are bigger or stronger and I wonder why I can't look like that. I see kids who have the newest and best toys and games and feel bad that I don't have them too. But when I focus on other people and their stuff, I lose sight of the things You have given me. Help me not be jealous of others. And help me never try to make someone else jealous of the things I have. May I be thankful for who You made me to be. May I wake up each morning thankful for simply waking up.

Think about it:

When you look at other people's blessings, do you think of how God has blessed you? What are some of the things you can be thankful for today?

HONESTY

*Keep your tongue from sin and
your lips from speaking lies.*
PSALM 34:13

Lord, honesty is important. If I want to be believed when it matters, I need to be honest all the time. People use lots of excuses to justify lying, but none of them justifies dishonesty. Lord, if I've done something I am not supposed to do, give me the boldness to admit my sin and seek to make things right. Keep me from lying and adding sin to sin to hide what I've done. I can't hide my sin from You anyway, so there is no point in lying about it. I pray that I would never try to get someone else in trouble by lying about them. Keep me honest.

Think about it:

Do you think lying is ever okay if you get away with it? Do you trust people who have lied to you in the past? How can you become a trustworthy person?

GIRLS AND BROKEN HEARTS

He heals those who have a broken heart.
He heals their sorrows.
PSALM 147:3

Lord, girls puzzle me. They are so different from me, but I can't help but like them, even though I don't understand them. But it hurts when I like a girl and she doesn't like me in the same way. I know I'm too young for a grown-up style relationship, but it would be nice to have a girl like me. You are the God who made boys and girls different from one another, and You are the Savior the world rejected, so I'm sure that You know what I'm talking about. When I'm sad and feeling alone, please come near to me. Change my perspective and draw me out of myself. Thank You for loving me more than any girl ever could.

Think about it:

Who can you trust enough to talk to when you are feeling alone? How can you change your focus when you're thinking too much about girls?

WHAT THE HEART IS FULL OF

"Good comes from a good man because of the riches he has in his heart. Sin comes from a sinful man because of the sin he has in his heart. The mouth speaks of what the heart is full of."
LUKE 6:45

Lord, when my heart is full of me and the things I want, I end up doing all kinds of things I regret. But when my heart is filled with You, I find it much easier to do the right things. It is easier to be generous when I'm not thinking about how much I love having stuff for myself. It is easier to be kind when I'm not focused on what I can get from other people. Lord, help me be a good man with a rich heart who does good because it is a natural thing for me to do.

Think about it:

Do you find it hard to do good things
for other people? Do your words
match what's in your heart?

Be THANKFUL FOR TODAY

This is the day that the Lord has made.
Let us be full of joy and be glad in it.
PSALM 118:24

Heavenly Father, thank You for this day. May Your joy live in me and through me today no matter what happens. Let me be glad for the simple blessings You give me. Thank You for air to breathe, water to drink, food to eat, work to do, and people to bless. Help me focus my thoughts and energy on other people more than myself. Let them see the joy I have today and realize that it comes from You. Thank You for giving me good days when things are easy. Thank You for giving me hard days when I need to draw closer to You. Thank You for this day. Whether my day is easy or hard, I know it is Yours and that You have made it for me.

Think about it:

What things do you take joy in? How do you remain thankful on hard days?

SCHOOL DISCIPLINE

O sons, hear the teaching of a father.
Listen so you may get understanding.
PROVERBS 4:1

All-knowing God, my teachers aren't like You. They don't know everything, even if they act like they do. But they know more than me. Help me not act like I know everything. Help me listen when they teach. Help me to not distract other kids in my class. Lord, I know I could face consequences when I don't listen, when I talk back to my teacher, or when I distract other kids. I pray that my actions would show my respect for those in leadership rather than fear of discipline. And if I face punishment from the school for my actions or attitudes, I pray that You would change my heart and my behavior so I can hear what I'm being taught.

Think about it:

Is there something or someone that makes it hard to listen to your teacher's instruction in school? What can you do to be nice to your teacher?

FEAR OF LOSING A PARENT

"Are not two small birds sold for a very small piece of money? And yet not one of the birds falls to the earth without your Father knowing it. God knows how many hairs you have on your head. So do not be afraid. You are more important than many small birds."
MATTHEW 10:29–31

Father God, I know I'm important to You, but sometimes I'm still afraid for the things that could happen to me and my family. Please replace my fear of losing my parents with Your love. Rather than being afraid for what might happen, may I trust You to handle things so that I can enjoy this moment. You know what is best for me, and You have the power to make the best things happen.

Think about it:

What do you do when you feel afraid of hard things that could happen to you and your family, especially your parents? Do you trust that God will take care of you no matter what?

CARING FOR THE EARTH

Then the Lord God took the man and put him in the garden of Eden to work the ground and care for it.
GENESIS 2:15

Creator God, You made this beautiful world I live in, and You made mankind to take care of it. Even before sin entered the world, You gave us a job to do. You gave it to us before we sinned, so it must have been a good job. Lord, help me to do my part to take care of the world You made. Help me take practical steps to make this world better by using resources responsibly and not littering. Help me love Your creation like You do.

Think about it:

How important is it to you that you help care for the earth you live on? What are some practical things you can do to care for the planet?

DOING YOUR BEST WORK

Whatever work you do, do it with all your heart.
Do it for the Lord and not for men.
COLOSSIANS 3:23

Lord, I pray that my work would be pleasing to You. It would be nice if my parents and teachers praised the work I do, but it is even better when You are pleased with it. May I always put in the effort needed to do quality work. And if I'm just learning how to do something, help me pay attention so I can learn quickly. I know I wouldn't be happy if someone gave me a half-baked meal, and I know You don't take joy in half-baked efforts either. I pray that I will finish each job with the satisfaction that only comes when I've done my best for You.

Think about it:

When you work, do you always give it your best effort? How can you make sure you always work like you're working for God Himself?

LIFE THAT LASTS FOREVER

"For God so loved the world that He gave His only Son. Whoever puts his trust in God's Son will not be lost but will have life that lasts forever."
JOHN 3:16

Trustworthy God, thank You for sending Your Son to the world. Thank You for accepting me into Your family and giving me life that lasts forever. Lord, help me be bold enough to share Your loving gift of life with my friends. I pray that each one would come to know You and put their trust in Your Son. The alternative to accepting Your love is an eternity without You. I pray that my friends would realize, like I do, that no one can get to You through their own efforts. Help me introduce others to Your love in a loving way.

Think about it:

Can you think of a friend who needs to know Jesus as Savior? How can you introduce that person to Jesus in a loving way?

ATTITUDES TOWARD PARENTS

The eye that makes fun of a father and hates to obey a mother will be picked out by the ravens of the valley and eaten by the young eagles.
PROVERBS 30:17

Lord, help me control my attitude when my parents talk to me. I may not agree with everything they say, but they love me and want what is best for me. May my eyes not roll when I think they are wrong. May I not sneer when I disagree. Lord, help me be respectful and wait for the opportunity to tell my parents what I am thinking. Help me see their point of view in the same way I would like them to see mine. Help me to always be respectful, not only because it is important to my parents, but also because it is important to You.

Think about it:

In what ways have you shown your parents disrespect in the past? What can you do, both in your words and your body language, to show them respect?

LOOKING FORWARD

No, Christian brothers, I do not have that life yet. But I do one thing. I forget everything that is behind me and look forward to that which is ahead of me. My eyes are on the crown. I want to win the race and get the crown of God's call from heaven through Christ Jesus.
PHILIPPIANS 3:13–14

Lord, my life is just getting started, but that doesn't mean I haven't already made some bad choices. I pray that my eyes would be on the track ahead of me rather than on the mistakes behind me. Keep my eyes on the goal ahead. Remind me that I don't run alone. You made the track. You taught me how to run. My strength comes from You. Lord, help me be a consistent runner, always moving forward at a steady pace toward You.

Think about it:

What are some temptations that draw your eyes away from the prize God has for you? How can you keep from looking behind you during the race?

FEAR OF FAILURE

For a man who is right with God falls seven times, and rises again, but the sinful fall in time of trouble.
PROVERBS 24:16

Perfect God, I can't live up to Your perfection. I will always fall short. But being right with You isn't about how many times I fall, but how many times I rise again. Lord, don't let my fear of failure keep me from getting back up. You have a habit of using people who don't seem qualified to do Your work. Moses wasn't a skilled speaker. Peter was kind of a meathead. Paul persecuted the church. But You get more glory when the success is obviously Yours. Help me rise again each time I fall. Use me despite my past failures, or maybe even because of them.

Think about it:

Does the fear of failure ever keep you from trying to do something worthwhile? Do you think your failures make it so God can't use you? What does the verse above say about that?

SPECIAL-NEEDS KIDS

"Then the King will say, 'For sure, I tell you, because you did it to one of the least of My brothers, you have done it to Me.'"
MATTHEW 25:40

Lord, I pray that I would see all people like You see them, no matter how different they look from me. Kids with special needs are made in Your image, just like I am. And though they may operate at a different speed or in a different way, help me to treat them with the love and respect all Your image bearers deserve. Give me sensitivity in how I talk about—and to—kids who are different from me. May I see their needs and help to fill them the best I can without making them feel helpless. Give me a heart that is kind to all.

Think about it:

How do you treat kids who have special needs? What is something kind you could do when you see someone who is different from you?

POP CULTURE

*Do not love the world or anything in the world.
If anyone loves the world, the Father's love is not
in him. For everything that is in the world does not
come from the Father. The desires of our flesh and
the things our eyes see and want and the pride of this
life come from the world. The world and all its desires
will pass away. But the man who obeys God and
does what He wants done will live forever.*

1 JOHN 2:15–17

Lord, I hear people talking about what shows and movies they watch, which musicians they listen to, and what clothes they like. People like to talk about what is popular right now. Popular stuff isn't necessarily bad, but I know I shouldn't pay more attention to what's popular than I pay to You. May I do Your will without worrying if it is popular.

Think about it:

What can you do to make sure your focus is on God and not on what's popular with your friends?

ENCOURAGING YOUR CHURCH LEADERS

*He who is taught God's Word should share
the good things he has with his teacher.*
GALATIANS 6:6

Lord, thank You for people who care about Your Word. I pray that You will bless my church's leadership and help them teach the Bible well, through both their words and their actions. Help me be an encouragement to these leaders as they work to bring Your Word to my community. When You teach me something new and exciting from Your Word, remind me to share it with my pastor. Lord, help me to pay attention when Your Word is taught at church. Help me apply it to my life so I have good things to share at church. I pray that others would encourage my church's leaders as well, so that their joy at doing Your will is strengthened.

Think about it:

What specific thing have you learned recently
at church? What are some ways that you
can encourage your church leaders?

FeeLING HopeLeSS

"God will take away all their tears. There will be
no more death or sorrow or crying or pain.
All the old things have passed away."
REVELATION 21:4

God of my salvation, sometimes I feel empty and alone. I don't feel joy or happiness. I don't have hope that things will get better. I know in my head and my heart that You are with me, but that knowledge sometimes doesn't help me feel better. Lord, You never promised me a life of sunshine and rainbows all the time, but I pray that You will help me feel better. Thank You for Your promises that await me beyond this life. When I feel hopeless in this passing world, remind me that I'm going to a place where You will dry my tears and there will be no more death or sorrow or crying or pain.

Think about it:

What does God promise after this life?
Who here on earth can you talk
to when you are feeling hopeless?

BOREDOM

Being lazy makes one go into a deep sleep,
and a lazy man will suffer from being hungry.
PROVERBS 19:15

Lord, save me from my boredom. Nothing sounds like fun right now. I need somewhere useful to put my energy, something worthwhile to work toward. I know that You have prepared good things for me to do, but what are they? Lord, give me some direction. I have no desire to be lazy. Taking naps only moves the clock forward without accomplishing anything. I pray for inspiration, not just amusement. If I've been avoiding responsibilities, help me remember them so I can finally do them. If there are kind things I can do for others, help me think of them. Lord, take my mind off myself and my boredom and turn it toward what You would have me do.

Think about it:

What things have you been putting off because you'd rather not do them? What is something nice you can make or do for someone you know?

CHOOSING HEROES WISELY

*He who walks with God, and whose words are good
and honest, he who will not take money received
from wrong-doing, and will not receive money given
in secret for wrong-doing, he who stops his ears from
hearing about killing, and shuts his eyes from looking
at what is sinful, he will have a place on high.*
ISAIAH 33:15–16

Praiseworthy God, may I choose my heroes wisely. While others look up to people who have special talents or money or power, help me admire someone who is known for putting You first. It isn't wrong to think athletes or actors are cool, but I want to model my life after someone whose character is strong and pure. May I grow up to become a person of good character myself, someone who isn't tempted by the things of this world.

Think about it:

What qualities do your heroes have? Do you
know someone in your family or church who
fits the description in the verses above?

TRUSTING GOD INSTEAD OF YOURSELF

Trust in the Lord with all your heart,
and do not trust in your own understanding.
PROVERBS 3:5

Father God, I know a lot of things, but I admit that I don't know it all. Trusting You should be the easiest thing in the world for me, but it isn't. You know everything and You have the power to do anything. And You love me. So why is it so hard to trust You? Lord, take away my belief that I can do things better on my own. My pride tells me that I should be able to do things without You, but I can't do *anything* without You. Teach me to listen to Your voice instead of my pride. You have a plan for my life, so help me to trust You and not myself.

Think about it:

What keeps you from trusting God?
Why do you believe that God's plan is
better than any you can make for yourself?

DEALING WITH CHANGE

Jesus Christ is the same yesterday
and today and forever.
HEBREWS 13:8

Lord, things change. People get sick. Friends move. What's popular one day is unpopular the next. Even my body seems different every morning. But You stay the same. You are always loving, always trustworthy, always forgiving. Thank You for staying the same when everything else is changing. When I am sad because things change, remind me that You always love me. When things don't seem like they are changing quickly enough, remind me that You are always in control. Lord, help me to be as steady as You are with the changes this life brings. May I always be committed to You and ready to do what You want, even if it means things will change for me.

Think about it:

How well do you deal with change? How does God always staying the same give you comfort?

WHEN PARENTS ARGUE

Be happy in your hope. Do not give up when trouble comes. Do not let anything stop you from praying.
ROMANS 12:12

Lord, be with my parents. It is hard when they aren't getting along. I pray that You would heal their relationship. Help them to know You and put You first. You tell me to be happy in my hope. My hope is that You will put Your love in my parents' hearts. May I remember to pray for them throughout the day. And if things don't get better for my parents' relationship, help me to keep praying for them anyway. The important thing for them is to know that You love them. I pray that You would use me to show them that You love them. Help them to put their own wants down and do what You want for them.

Think about it:

Do you pray for your parents' relationship when they're going through difficult times? What does the verse above say about that?

KNOWING GOD

*"This is life that lasts forever. It is to know You,
the only true God, and to know Jesus
Christ Whom You have sent."*
JOHN 17:3

Amazing God, there are times when I don't feel important. There are so many people in the world today, and many more who lived before me. Who am I that You should want to know me? But You have introduced Yourself through creation and invited me into a relationship with You through Your Son. You don't need me or anything I offer, but You want me. Lord, I pray that knowing You would never grow old for me. Thank You for reaching out for me. I can't truly live without living for You. When I am with You, I have the everlasting life You promised me, life even death can't overcome.

Think about it:

When you feel insignificant, how does it make you feel that the God who created everything wants to know you? How can you get to know God better?

WHEN THINGS DON'T GO YOUR WAY

The mind that thinks only of ways to please the sinful old self is fighting against God. It is not able to obey God's Laws. It never can.

ROMANS 8:7

Lord, it is frustrating when things don't go the way I want them to—like when I don't make the sports team, when we're not having the dinner I want, when I can't have the things other people have. When I'm disappointed, help me find comfort by taking my focus off myself and putting it on You. What You want for me is better than I deserve. Help me lose myself and my wants in You. Help me surrender myself to Your will for my life, even if it isn't what I would choose for myself.

Think about it:

Are you easily frustrated when things don't go your way? What helps you take the focus off yourself? What are some ways God has blessed you without giving you your way?

TAKING JOY IN THE RIGHT THINGS

Be happy in the Lord. And He will give you the desires of your heart.
PSALM 37:4

Generous God, may I take joy in You. The things I think will make me happy—money, popularity, relationships—can't give me lasting joy. That doesn't stop me from daydreaming about what I would do if I were a millionaire or how my life would be better if everyone liked me all the time. Lord, redirect my daydreams and make them thankful thoughts for the blessings You've already given me. You didn't promise to give me whatever my selfish heart desires—only that when my heart is satisfied with You alone, You will give me more of Yourself. Teach me to be happy with the things that make You happy. As I learn what those are, provide me with opportunities to work toward both Your happiness and mine.

Think about it:

What do you think makes God happy? Does your heart truly desire what God wants for you?

BeinG a LeaDeR

"Also, you should choose from the people able men who fear God, men of truth who hate to get things by doing wrong. Have these men rule over the people, as leaders of thousands, of hundreds, of fifties and of tens."
EXODUS 18:21

Lord, make me a good leader. I pray that people would see the direction I'm going and be inspired to follow, not because of me, but because I'm leading them toward You. If people do follow me, don't let it go to my head. Don't let me forget that no matter how many people I lead, You are still in charge. May my reputation be pure, and may I love doing the right thing so that when other people wonder whether they can follow my lead, they will see that I am a man of truth.

Think about it:

Are you ever asked to be a leader?
What kind of leader would you like to follow?
What kind of leader do you want to be?

NeveR Give UP

We are pressed on every side, but we still have room to move. We are often in much trouble, but we never give up. People make it hard for us, but we are not left alone. We are knocked down, but we are not destroyed.
2 CORINTHIANS 4:8–9

Merciful God, when the walls are closing in around me, remind me to look up. You are there with a way out of my problems. You will never leave me alone in my troubles. When my problems are with other people, help me find a way to repair the relationship. If my troubles are with school, give me understanding. And when my problems are self-inflicted, forgive me and help me make things right. Even if my problems are of my own making, You don't give up on me.

Think about it:

Do you ever want to just give up when things are tough? How do you think God can help you overcome your own problems?

SELF-SACRIFICE

*But God showed His love to us. While we
were still sinners, Christ died for us.*
ROMANS 5:8

Lord, it is never easy to give up what I want so someone else can have what they want. With my friends, it isn't as hard, because they like me and I like them. But it is a lot harder to give up what I want for people who don't like me. Everything inside me says it isn't fair. But You don't think like that. It would have been fair for You to not send a Savior and just leave people to their sin. But because You love everyone, even people who will never love You back, You gave us a way back to You through Your Son. Lord, help me follow Your example and love other people even when they won't love me back.

Think about it:

Can you think of someone right
now who you don't like very much?
How can you show that person love?

Genuine Concern

Be happy with those who are happy.
Be sad with those who are sad.
ROMANS 12:15

Lord, help me understand how people around me are feeling and thinking. Give me the sensitivity I need to love people where they are. When a person is happy about something, help me rejoice with them, even when they are happy about something I might be jealous about. When a person is sad, help me offer a shoulder to cry on, understanding that they might not want someone to try to fix it just yet. When a person is angry, help me understand why and whether I need to do something about it. When someone is afraid, help me encourage them. Lord, help me be genuine in my concern for people and helpful in my actions.

Think about it:

What are some clues you can use to find out how a person is feeling? Why is it important to understand why someone is feeling a certain way?

PARENTS, PUNISHMENTS, AND PERSPECTIVE

The stick and strong words give wisdom, but a child who gets his own way brings shame to his mother.
PROVERBS 29:15

Heavenly Father, sometimes my earthly parents drive me nuts. Sometimes I feel like they are out to get me and that they like making a big deal out of even my smallest mistakes. Lord, help me mend my relationship with my parents. Help me be respectful to them even when I don't feel like it. Help me accept punishment with grace and learn whatever I'm supposed to learn in the process. I don't want to bring shame on myself or my parents, so give me wisdom on how to interact with them when we aren't getting along. Help me understand things from their perspective. Help me avoid the mistakes that are bound to get me in trouble with them in the first place.

Think about it:

Do you ever feel like your parents are being unfair when they punish you? What wisdom can you get from being punished?

WORDS TO BUILD OTHERS UP

Each of us should live to please his neighbor.
This will help him grow in faith.
ROMANS 15:2

Perfect God, make me a good neighbor to the people around me. I pray that the words I speak would build them up, not tear them down. When people talk to me, I want their day to be better because of it. If I have a negative opinion of someone, help me keep it to myself and instead love them like You do. Keep me from listening to or passing on gossip. Help me know just what to say when someone is having a rough day. I pray that my words would be genuine and that people will grow in their faith because of the way that I speak.

Think about it:

Do you think people are happier after they talk with you? How can you use your words to build up others? How can you use your words to help people grow in their faith?

COMPASSION FOR OTHERS

God has chosen you. You are holy and loved by Him. Because of this, your new life should be full of loving-pity. You should be kind to others and have no pride. Be gentle and be willing to wait for others.
COLOSSIANS 3:12

Lord, I'm so glad that You chose me, even though I know I don't bring anything to this relationship. You just love me. I'm holy only because You set me apart for Yourself. Help me treat others with love, whether or not they bring anything of worth to the relationship. Give me patience and gentleness with those who need encouragement to accept Your love. Help me to lead them little bits at a time to You with words of comfort. Give me understanding and help me see the world they see so I can know the right way to bring them to You.

Think about it:

How much do you care about other people?
Do your actions show that you care?

FEELING LONELY

"Do not fear, for I am with you. Do not be afraid,
for I am your God. I will give you strength,
and for sure I will help you. Yes, I will hold you
up with My right hand that is right and good."
ISAIAH 41:10

Lord, sometimes I feel lonely. I know You say that You are always with me, but it is hard to feel You when I'm sitting by myself at lunch and no one sits next to me. Lord, give me the boldness to reach out to others when I feel lonely. Lift my spirits when I feel sad. Help me not to focus on myself and what I'm missing, but on others and how I'm blessed. Lord, help me not feel lonely today.

Think about it:

Do you often find yourself feeling lonely?
What can you do to reach out to other people
when you feel that way? What constructive
things can you do with time alone?

FORGIVING OTHERS

You must be kind to each other. Think of the other person. Forgive other people just as God forgave you because of Christ's death on the cross.
EPHESIANS 4:32

Righteous God, it is easy to get mad at someone who is being mean to me. It is easy to hold on to the pain the person caused me and let it live on in the back of my mind. In time, the pain will become bitterness and I might try to avoid that person altogether. I know You don't want me to hold on to my pain or let my bitterness grow. You are the God who fixes relationships. When I cause You pain, You don't hold it against me. Lord, when someone hurts me, help me to forgive that person. Take the pain out of my heart and show me how to restore the relationship.

Think about it:

Can you think of anyone who has hurt you and you haven't forgiven that person? What would it take for you to forgive that person?

ANGeR vs. PeACe

A man's anger does not allow
him to be right with God.
JAMES 1:20

God of peace, when people try to make me mad, keep me from giving them the satisfaction. Help me answer angry words with ones of peace and kindness. When I allow my anger to take control, I become someone I don't want to be. I stop caring about other people—other than how I can make them hurt. That isn't who You've called me to be, and it isn't how I can spread Your love to the world. Lord, when my anger gets in the way of Your love, it hurts my relationship with You. Keep me close. Help me shrug off insults. Help me resolve angry situations through the proper authorities instead of taking matters into my own hands. Replace my anger with Your peace.

Think about it:

What are some things that make you angry? What can you do the next time you encounter them?

OUR SAFE PLACE

God is our safe place and our strength.
He is always our help when we are in trouble.
PSALM 46:1

Lord, this world can be a dangerous place. Natural disasters, accidents, and wars happen all over. Schools and homes aren't even as safe as they should be. There is nowhere in the world I can go to feel completely safe. But that's okay, because You are my safe place. I am secure in Your love for me, regardless of what happens here on earth. That doesn't mean You aren't dangerous. You are the God of storms, and nothing is outside Your power. But You won't use Your power against me. This world may be a dangerous place, but I am safest in Your love. Thank You for keeping me safe until I get home to You.

Think about it:

Is anything outside of God's power? Do you
see God's love as a place of safety? How can
His love help you feel safe when you are scared?

WHEN YOU FIGHT WITH YOUR FRIENDS

But if you hurt and make it hard for each other,
watch out or you may be destroyed by each other.
GALATIANS 5:15

Lord, most of the time, my friends are great. But sometimes they drive me nuts. When that happens, help me find common ground with them. Help me talk to them and work things out. If I'm the reason we aren't getting along, I pray that You would change my heart and give me the humility I need to apologize. Me being stubborn about things doesn't fix the problem. If my friends are the problem, help me forgive them even before they ask for it. My friends and I work best as a team. I pray that the team would get back together quickly and that we'd be even stronger because we've been tested and worked it out.

Think about it:

What is getting in the way of you working things out with your friends? How can working things out this time make things better in the future?

TRUSTING GOD WITH THE FUTURE

Do not let your heart be jealous of sinners,
but live in the fear of the Lord always. For sure
there is a future and your hope will not be cut off.
PROVERBS 23:17–18

Faithful God, keep me from trying to take control away from You. I see other people doing whatever they want, and sometimes I wish I could do that too. And while it may be fun for a moment, getting my own way right now may mess things up in my future. Lord, You want what is best for me. The only way I can prosper, now and in the future, is to follow You and what You want for me. When things don't go the way that I want, help me trust You.

Think about it:

Do you ever feel jealous of people who do whatever they want? What would be the consequences if you did whatever you wanted? Have you given God control of your future?

CONFIDENCE

I can do all things because
Christ gives me the strength.
PHILIPPIANS 4:13

Lord, give me confidence in the right things. The world tells me I should believe in myself and that I can do anything I put my mind to. But I know I can't do anything by myself. Lord, help me depend on You and to believe I can do anything You give me the strength to do. Help me be confident, not because I can do things on my own, but because the things I am doing are things You will bless. I pray that I'll never be timid when it comes to serving You. May I use my skills and gifts with the confidence that comes from a pure heart. Whatever I do, help me do it for You and through You.

Think about it:

What are some things you can always do with confidence? How much can you do when you rely on your own strength?

READ AND PREACH AND TEACH

*Until I come, read and preach and
teach the Word of God to the church.*
1 TIMOTHY 4:13

Author God, thank You for giving me the Bible. Help me read it faithfully. May I learn more about You and love You more each time I read it. Help me to tell other people the things I learn when I read so they can love You more too. Lord, even though I'm not grown up, I pray that I could still teach people about You. Help me understand Your Word, so I don't tell people the wrong things. Even though the words stay the same, I pray that each reading will be fresh to me. If the Bible ever seems boring to me, change my heart and bring me closer to Yours.

Think about it:

What have you learned from the Bible that you can tell someone about today? How can you make sure God's Word is fresh for you each time you read it?

THE NARROW DOOR

"Go in through the narrow door. The door is wide and the road is easy that leads to hell. Many people are going through that door."
MATTHEW 7:13

Worthy God, when I see an easy way ahead, open my eyes and help me see the path I'm on as You see it. If things are easy because I'm taking the wrong path, help me find the narrow door to the right one. Living for You won't be easy by the world's standards. When I place control of my life into Your hands, I don't know what hard things I'll go through, but I know You won't leave me alone. Hold my hand as I walk that narrow way. When I wish for an easier path, give me Your strength. Thank You for keeping the narrow door open for me.

Think about it:

Do you make the hard choice to follow God even when life is easy? How can you help your friends stay on the right path with you?

HEAVEN

They will see His face and His name will be written on
their foreheads. There will be no night there. There will
be no need for a light or for the sun. Because the Lord
God will be their light. They will be leaders forever.
REVELATION 22:4–5

Lord, thank You for putting Your name on my fore-
head. I pray that it would be as obvious to the people around me here on earth as it will be in heaven
that I belong to You. May Your light shine through
my words, my actions, and even my face. I can't
wait to get to heaven and see all the beautiful sights
and meet all of Your followers who have gone before me. For now, though, I pray that I would be useful for You while I'm still in this world.

Think about it:

How can your friends and family members
know that you belong to Jesus? What
are some ways that you can help bring
others into God's kingdom on earth?

THE CONCLUSION OF THE MATTER

The last word, after all has been heard, is: Honor God and obey His Laws. This is all that every person must do.
ECCLESIASTES 12:13

Everlasting God, You gave me the Bible so I could get to know You. You gave me Your laws so I could know what things are important to You. The instructions are pretty clear. I'm supposed to honor You and love others. Lord, help me do that today. May I see the good things You have prepared for me to do, and may I choose to do them with a good attitude. I pray that my words and actions bring honor and glory to You, not me. Help me trust You with the things that happen today. Thank You for loving me, no matter what.

Think about it:

In what ways can you bring honor to God today?
Which of His laws is hardest for you to obey?
What do you think God wants you to do today?

SCRIPTURE INDEX